START WITH ONE

START WITH ONE

A Journey Through Homosexuality, Christianity, Societal Prejudices,
and the Will to Prevail

Adam Mastroianni

Edited by Blue Square Writers' Studio in Denver, CO.
www.bluesquarewriters.com

Photography courtesy of Aidan Mackerracher Photography.
www.monstamunch.com

Cover design by Elizabeth at Creative Allure Design.
www.creativealluredesign.com

A very special thank you to my good friends Deb & Bill Kelly at the Kelly Family Cuidiú Foundation, who have so graciously offered to help sponsor this project's outreach.

ISBN-13: 978 – 1530773206
ISBN-10: 1530773202

Dedicated to my ever-loving and supportive family: Mom, Dad, Tiffany, Grandma Bernie, Logan, and my two angels in the sky, Grandpa Tony and Grandma Nina

Contents

Preface *1*

Childhood and Background 3

A Homophobic World 9

Making One Difficult Decision & Stalling Another 13

Self-Deception in Germany 17

Hacked 23

High School Uncertainties 27

Preparing for College 33

Finding Christianity 39

UBUNTU and the Winds of Change 43

Lake Chautauqua Lutheran Center 49

Freshman Year at Siena 53

Taking a Risk 59

A Non-Welcoming Bible Study 65

Returning to LCLC 69

The Dilemma Awaits 75

Senior High Week 79

Junior Year: Changing Course 85

A Breath of Freedom 87

Crush; Crushed 93

Stepping Back – Easter 2006 101

First Relationship 105

A Crack in the Planet 109

Setting My Sights upon Italy 117

Ti Amo, Ti Amo Sempre 127

Returning to Europe 131

Defining My Purpose 137

Shedding Back Another Layer 141

Coming Out to Family and Friends.............................147

Unwelcomed..157

Homosexuality in the Bible..161

Venturing into Healthcare and Colorado 171

Stepping out on a Limb That Broke............................177

Tackling the Business World as a Gay Man 181

The Loss of a Friendship 185

Meeting Logan 189

Gay Marriage Legalized in Colorado and the Nation 199

The Adventure of a Lifetime 205

A Call for Action 211

Conclusion 215

Appendix A 219

    Need Help? 219

    Want To Get Involved?...221

References 224

START WITH ONE

Preface

I struggled deeply with my identity throughout my formative, adolescent years. A black cloud looked to hang prominently above my future. Amidst the hardships of living a constant lie and facing internal battles with depression and self-acceptance, I realized that I had to approach my life one day at a time. During the more than ten years of work that I put into this book, I discovered that it's never too late to follow my heart and to keep hope for a better tomorrow by doing so.

My mission and passion in creating this book was to reach even just one person in need of a message of hope. I also wrote this work to provide insight and understanding into one of the most misunderstood and prejudiced topics within society. In an effort to help spread awareness, for each book that is sold, one free copy will be donated. Along with a list of lesbian, gay, bisexual and transgender (LGBT) educational resources, the donated books will be distributed to LGBT-friendly high schools, churches, homeless shelters and organizations nationwide. If one person's life can be changed, then sharing my story will be well worth it.

Childhood and Background

I don't recall when I first "knew." In fact, I'm not one of the people that can pinpoint the exact timeframe. My first recollection of the word gay happened around the age of five. One of my relatives insinuated that I might be. I didn't quite understand what it meant, but I knew that whatever she implied was definitely a bad thing. Others around me said, "Don't say that," and "No, he's not." Her statement confused me as a young child. I was just being myself. I did enjoy helping my Mom with gardening, and I took an interest in her cooking. However, I still loved and played all sports, and I built LEGO and K'NEX structures just the same.

As a seven year old, I felt certain attractions that I kept to myself. Each year, my sister Tiffany and I attended a summer camp in upstate New York. We played just about every sport in the book. I met my first crush there. My favorite counselors happened to both be guys, Jamie and Bill. I really liked Bill, and vied for his attention at camp. He sported cut off athletic t-shirts and always wore the same worn down baseball hat. I missed him every time I left camp. One weekend, Jamie and Bill surprised us by stopping by our house. They swung Tiffany and I on our tire swing, and we hugged them tightly. I jumped up for a piggyback ride and refused to jump back off. I knew I was a bit different, but as a kid, you think everyone probably is, and everyone is just hiding it too.

The following year, my parents picked up and left our hometown to venture into the entrepreneurial world in Schenectady, NY. My Mom, Dad, sister and I set out on a new adventure as a family. We followed in the footsteps of my Italian grandparents who had successfully started and ran multiple businesses in America. My parents began the Glenville Sportplex, an outdoor family-fun center with mini-golf, batting cages, bankshot basketball, bumper cars, go-karts, a driving range, and a full service snack bar. I handed out putters, emptied arcade games of quarters, mopped bathrooms, and helped to repair batting cage machines, all after a day of fourth grade. My sister and I quickly learned both the value and reward of hard work while building and operating a business from the ground up.

Most of my friends' parents tried to ground their children in cement, and left no room for error or self-actualization. My parents raised us differently. They grounded us in mud. Mud that was thin enough to maneuver our way through learning life's lessons first-hand, but thick enough to keep us grounded in our morals and the importance of family, love, and faith. My parents always took this approach. They stressed the importance of letting me find myself through my own unique journey, while still having solid walls and a foundation up to support me.

When hormones and physical attractions came into the picture just a few short years later, life became confusing and immediately lost its simplicity and transparency. My male friends discussed their growing attractions towards girls. I experienced quite the opposite. I found myself innately attracted to guys, not girls, and I didn't understand what that meant. In my early years as a preteen and teen, I thought it might be a stage or a phase that would soon pass. It didn't seem to be normal. Nobody else seemed to share the same problem as me. The older I got and the more everyone's testosterone kicked in, the quicker I realized that my natural attractions weren't fading away.

In my significantly populated Italian-American hometown with a commonly themed "macho man" mentality, people made it clear that being gay was weird, gross, and unacceptable. Kids at school made fun of others by calling them faggots. I heard the expression "that's gay" probably 50 times a day. My hometown and general society did not understand LGBT people. The media lacked information or resources pertaining to the gay community. It was a completely taboo topic. I felt alone, isolated, and that something may have in fact been wrong with me as a person.

My extended Christian family around me preached that gay people were unacceptable in the eyes of God. My aunts and uncles proclaimed that gay people needed to repent and rebuke themselves from their sinful ways. One day I overheard my cousins talking about a gay teenager at their school. My aunt scolded him, "Don't you talk about that filth in this household, do you hear me?" He obliged. I quickly learned the urgency of keeping my secret safe.

Convinced to fit in, I pretended to like a girl Eliza in middle school. We dated. I knew what I "should" be doing, after watching plenty of movies and television my whole life. I had ample ideas on what to do and exactly how to do so. I bought her flowers. I walked her to and from class. I wrote little notes and left them in her locker. We spent each night on the telephone chatting and saying our goodnights before bed. Subsequently, I thought she would like me more if she saw me play baseball.

I invited Eliza to one of my games. In the bottom of the ninth inning, I walked towards home plate with my metal Louisville Slugger bat in hand. The bases were loaded and we were down by two runs. The pitcher threw his first pitch and I heard "strike!" yelled loudly from the umpire behind home plate. I glanced over at Eliza and nerves ran through my body. As the pitcher wound up for his next delivery, a fastball came rushing towards me in my sweet spot, high and inside. I swung for the fences, and that's exactly where that ball headed. Deep in left field, I saw the outfielder scrambling to back up to the fence. But the ball had already passed him and cleared it. I hit a grand slam.

As I rounded the bases and headed towards home plate, I looked towards the bleachers to see Eliza's reaction. I thought, "I hope this impresses her enough to keep her as my girlfriend." I wanted so desperately to fit in and be liked, and to have a normal life that so many of my friends around me seemed to have. I wanted to hold on to Eliza to ensure that I wasn't exposed as different from my peers.

My team celebrated with a pizza party. I brought Eliza along for the ride, and proudly introduced her as my girlfriend. My family congratulated me before bed on a great game. In the confines of my private room, sorrow replaced my joy. I prayed to God to change me and make me normal like those around me. I cried. I didn't know if I had done something wrong to deserve my feelings, or if there was a way to fix me either. I wished it all just went away.

I didn't want to be gay. I never choose to be gay. I just... was. Being gay felt as natural to me as anything else did. I kept up my routine of faking my external happiness around others, and withholding my internal confusion and distress. Discussing my sexuality wasn't an option. I deeply feared the repercussions that coming out would have led to at home, in school, on the athletic fields, or within the religious realm.

A Homophobic World

Not a single country in the world allowed gay marriage in 1997. News coverage did not support gay rights. The television and film industry did not have any gay or lesbian characters; no actor ventured such a risk. Ellen DeGeneres broke that mold. She felt an absolute need to be true to herself. She came out by having the main character "Ellen" of her hit TV show face the same issue. Ellen explained her thought process at the time, "Would I still be famous, would they still love me if they knew I was gay? And my fear was that no, no they wouldn't, and then it made me feel ashamed that I was hiding something. It made me feel ashamed that I couldn't feel honest and really be who I am."[1] After her revelation, the infamous Time Magazine cover with Ellen's picture read simply, "Yep, I'm Gay."

I anxiously watched the news. I didn't yet identify as a gay male because I didn't fully understand what that meant. I knew that something was different with me, but I still hoped that the stage would pass. Ellen's story revealed a first ever sliver of hope into a possible explanation. "Maybe being 'gay' was a thing," I thought to myself. My 12 year-old mind pondered the question, but I kept my thoughts and opinions strictly to myself. I watched the media blast her name and her career. The religious right condemned her. People in school expressed their disgust and called her hurtful names.

After building up her career, it took an abrupt and serious downfall. The network began to show a "parental warning" for content on the show beforehand. Big advertisers pulled their money. Ellen received multiple death threats and bomb threats. One newscaster warned parents of exposing their children to the story, as if being gay was an infection that others could catch. I kept my mouth shut regarding any feelings of empathy or concern. I wanted nothing to do with the word "gay" and all of its negative associations. I concluded that it wasn't me. I just hadn't worked hard enough to fix my feelings of attraction yet.

The following year, national news caught my eye once again. In 1998, Matthew Shepard was brutally beaten and murdered in an anti-gay hate crime in Laramie, Wyoming. Matthew suffered fractures to his skull and severe brain damage from the attack. His attackers left him tied to a fence, where he remained for 18 hours, until he was discovered by a passing cyclist. Rushed to the hospital, his injuries proved too severe. Matthew died a few days later while on life support. He was 21 years old.

Eighteen hundred miles away in New York, I cried for Matthew's unjust murder. As a 13 year-old, my natural attractions remained. I increasingly sensed that I too might belong to this group of gay people. I despised the feeling. I refused to admit it. Internally, I empathized with someone whom I had never known. I asked God to give peace to his parents. I begged and prayed for God to change me. I didn't want to be punished like Matthew for something I felt I never had any control over.

Reverend Fred Phillips, leader of the WestBoro Baptist Church, led a picket at Matthew's funeral. His supporters hoisted "No Tears For Queers" and "God Hates Fags" posters. Picketers shouted at friends and family of Matthew "Fags burn in hell," and "Thank God for killing gays." My heart ached for Matthew and his family. My confusion and absolute disgust grew with the Reverend's mean-spirited hate group. "Wasn't Matthew still just a human?" I thought to myself, "How can members of a *church* be so heartless and absolutely cruel?"

I watched Judy and Dennis Shepard's emotional interviews. I lost my innocence that year. I lost my naïve belief that the world was always a good place. The images of the protestors burned a memory into my mind. I thought, "Just what would happen if I ever ran into this group on the street?" I feared my life to come out. My innate desire for honesty and self-exploration didn't overtake my fears of getting publicly shamed, hurt, or killed.

I relentlessly tried to change my sexuality. I prayed for it to happen every single night. I found as many pictures as I could of good-looking women in magazines and stared at them each night. I befriended more girls in high school and figured I just hadn't found the right one yet. I involved myself in discussions with my older teammates on my baseball team, and forced interest in their stories and conversations about girls. I never wanted my parents to have to face what the Shepard's did. I desired to provide them with what I thought all families wanted: a straight, and normal son.

Making One Difficult Decision & Stalling Another

When I was 16 years old, I decided that I was no longer going to play baseball – something I had done since as long as I could remember. At the time I stopped playing baseball, people in every aspect of my life could not believe it. My decision came off the heels of me placing in the top five in the country with a promising future ahead. I found myself constantly explaining why I was giving it up and it became absolutely exhausting. I made up excuses like not getting along with the coach, wanting to play other sports, and placing blame upon the increasing politics behind the game. All had some hints of truth to them, but in all honesty, I knew in my heart that I didn't have the passion within me to continue playing. I went to bed each night thinking of how I would no longer be following in my Dad's footsteps, and how much I must be disappointing him.

As a kid, my Dad had an absolute God-given talent and he was on track towards the Major Leagues. However, one evening while he was driving home, a fire truck on the highway forgot to put its flashers on, and he swerved off the road to avoid it. He flipped his car over multiple times, and crushed his spine in three different places. Miraculously, only a couple of millimeters separated him from lifelong paralysis. He spent the next four months in a half body cast, and another full year in therapy learning how to walk and tie his shoes again. God unveiled a different plan for his life's journey.

Since my Dad's dream of reaching the Majors got cut short, and since I luckily got his talents and skills, I felt that I should be utilizing them accordingly.

My Dad and I talked through my decision for weeks, but I ultimately stuck with it. He remained supportive, but I knew that watching me quit was extremely difficult on him. As hard as it was to go through, my Dad made it well known that he still loved and supported me. When I appeared overly stressed about the decision, he would lighten the mood with a joke. As a 16-year old kid, I learned the importance of making decisions for myself, staying true to myself, and that I couldn't go through life trying to please others. If only dealing with the gay issue would have been that direct.

I grew to realize that coming out one day was perhaps inevitable. I thought about perhaps confronting the issue at this time. Being gay wasn't going away. As hard as that truth was to face, I was still nowhere near ready to face the facts with myself or fully accept them either. I feared a similar reaction from my hometown and extended family's buzz after I quit playing baseball. I didn't want to cause that big of a stir or disruption in my personal or academic life again. On a scale of 1-10, my comfort and confidence level with my own sexuality rated a "2" at best. I felt most content keeping my secret locked up in the safe haven of my own mind.

No one suspected that I was gay. I walked, talked, played sports, and did whatever else any "normal" guy did. The only way people would have known back then was if I told them first-hand, or if I wrote it on my forehead with a sharpie. If I came out, I needed to be prepared to defend and speak to it to those around me. The news would have spread like wildfire. Part of me still felt that I could work upon changing this aspect about myself. Throughout my remaining years in high school I desperately continued to see if it would go away.

Self-Deception in Germany

During middle school, I followed in my sister's shoes and opted to take German instead of the more popular offerings like Spanish and French. I continued to do so throughout high school. After having four years' study of the language, some of my classmates and I traveled to Germany as part of an exchange program. With my application, funding, and a lot of paperwork including going to get my first official passport, I headed to Germany with a group of 20 of my fellow American classmates.

As a 16 year-old closeted gay teenager whose face was half covered in acne, my self confidence suffered around the time of the trip. Although I appeared to hold myself confidently, on the inside I felt pretty far from that. I worked hard to make sure that I protected myself from ever letting my secret out. I constantly analyzed my expressions, interactions, and observations of others' reactions of me to ensure that I was never perceived as gay.

After the long flight to Germany, our exchange students greeted us at the airport. We took a long bus ride as a group, and quickly discovered that their English was much better than our German. From the seating on the bus, it became clear who the popular kids were from the German group, and the same went for us. These kids quickly huddled into the back of the bus. I found myself in the middle between this gathering in the back, and the outcasts that sat up front near the chaperones and teachers. The German students provided insight into their own classmates that sat up front. Their conversations then shifted towards Thomas, a seemingly nice kid, and pretty quiet in his overall demeanor. One of my male American friends identified of having Thomas as his exchange student. A German girl then warned him in her thick accent,

"You might want to sleep with your ass against the wall!"

Everyone laughed, myself included, mainly so that I could fit in. As the German students continued to rumor, they kept making jokes about Thomas. I nonchalantly turned back in my seat and put some music on. I recalled various statements from elementary school onwards, like those about Thomas, which forced me deeper into masking my identity. It seemed that I would be judged, ridiculed, and made fun of no matter where I went if I revealed myself. A happy future for me appeared impossible.

Our host families greeted us in the city of Frankfurt, and we departed with our exchange students to their respective homes. Over the next ten days, we attended classes at a German school, saw various local cultural shows, and saw many beautiful cities and quaint villages around Frankfurt. With peer and societal pressures surrounding me in a new environment, I subconsciously placed an increased spotlight of scrutiny upon myself.

One day, I found myself giving in to one of the German girl's glances at me, and hints that she wanted to be more than just friends. I regularly befriended girls at that stage in my life, and if I sensed that they liked me, I slowly put distance between us. However, a few people in my class and the German class asked what was going on with Julia and me. Julia was a very pretty girl with long blond hair and had an athletic, yet petite figure.

While kicking around a soccer ball one afternoon, we wrestled down to the ground and burst out into laughter. As we both lay down on the grass in the field I thought, "Oh, is this when I am supposed to kiss someone?" I became cognizant that everyone observed our interactions. It was awkward to completely fake interest in her, but I desired to try. Though we continued to flirt with one another that day, we didn't kiss.

Subsequently, over the following week, another girl started giving me that same vibe as well, Sarah. Sarah was different though. She had shoulder length black hair and fair skin, and was very straightforward in her demeanor. While at one of the student's house while in the basement, she came up to me and bluntly said,

"If you want to fuck, we can go upstairs."

I didn't know how to reply. She said it with such a straight face and lack of emotion, trying to evoke my response or interest to take her up on the offer at that moment. I blushed, turned around, and walked quickly in the opposite direction. As awkward as this situation was, a couple of my female friends overheard this interaction and hilarity soon took over. We cracked up in the corner and shook our heads in disbelief at Sarah's statement.

The friendship between Julia and I continued. We should have progressed to more than friends judging by our ease of interactions at school and after school during our group hangouts.

Even my exchange student's parents asked me what was going on with us. I smiled and politely changed the topic. After an evening gathering, my exchange student's dad picked up a few of us. Julia and I sat in the backseat. We held hands on the way to the car that night, and the father gave me a smile and a wink of approval when he saw this.

For the entire drive home, she wouldn't let go of my hand. We massaged each other's hands and lower arms. When we stopped at her house to drop her off, there was but one thing left to do: kiss. The car stopped, and even with my exchange student and his dad in the front seat, Julia made it clear that she was not going anywhere until she got what she wanted. I leaned over to give her a kiss. I wanted to get it over as fast as possible, so I went in for a quick peck. That didn't work. She went in with an open mouth and held the back of my head with her hand. She shoved her tongue into my mouth while trying to elicit the same response from me. The situation repulsed me and I wanted to puke. But yet, like a trained actor, I knew exactly what to do. I returned the act, and then helped her out of the car. I received the "oooohh" noises from the front of the car. Their response made me feel manly, which puzzled me. At the same time I felt like I betrayed not only myself but also her, and feared the next time we saw one another.

I went to bed that night confused with my actions, as a slew of emotions took over me. I failed miserably in my attempt to force myself straight. This is what I thought I was supposed to do, but it couldn't have felt any more wrong. I kissed a pretty, athletic, outgoing girl, but it didn't matter. Inevitably, she was still just a girl. Julia would have been a great fit for me, if I had an even slight attraction towards women. Yet all I saw when I looked at her, no matter how hard I tried, was just a friend.

The next few times I saw Julia, I could tell in her eyes that she expected to continue where we left off. I found myself absolutely unable to. She became visibly disappointed and sad, as her efforts were unmatched in trying to spend additional time with me. I felt like a complete jerk while trying to find a nice way to let her down. I resorted to my familiar routine of pushing away a girl that liked me to protect both her and myself.

Hacked

When I started to explore the Internet as a teenager, like most boys post-puberty, I ran across things once in a while that sparked my interest. Latin pop singer Ricky Martin was one of them. I thought he was good looking, and the way he moved made me want to keep watching his music videos. One day while watching some of his videos, I followed a trail of links on the web pages. I found myself about to click on a Playgirl website link. I recalled how my male friends at school talked about their Playboy magazines, and pleasantly discovered that there was another site directed at a completely different audience.

I feared visiting the website on my family's computer. I didn't want to get discovered. However, my heart raced and my adrenaline pumped at a level it never had before. I looked the other way as I clicked the link, almost to tell myself, "You landed upon this by mistake." I trusted the website on good faith that I had to input a credit card online to prove that I was 18 years or older. With my Mom's credit card information, I gained access. I quickly understood why the boys at school got so excited over their Playboy magazines. It was natural and intrinsic; the same way that looking at Playgirl was for me in that very moment.

About a month after my online discovery, my Mom called my sister and I to the top of our staircase. She looked up at us both as we stood on the small landing. She held out a piece of paper from the bottom of the stairs and asked,

"Do either of you know why there is a $30 charge from Playgirl.com on my credit card bill?!"

Without even giving my sister a second to reply, I threw my hand upon my chest out of 'shock' and yelled, "Tiffany!" She looked at my Mom and I with a face of complete surprise. She proclaimed that she didn't do it. My Mom said, "So you had no part in this?" Tiff replied, "No."

"Adam, did you have anything to do with this?"

"No," I said, in a voice that suggested I was appalled at the insinuation. My poor sister. Not only did I take it upon myself to fast-talk myself out of just about anything, I was also viewed as the angel child, the baby, and I usually got my way more than her. With both of our absolute denials regarding the inquisition, my Mom let the subject rest. Phew.

Back to Ricky Martin. In the day or two following my online searches, I held a certain amount of discontent within myself. I knew enough to clear the browsing history and do a few more tricks to hide my mouse clicks, but I still felt completely uneasy. A few days later, my computer savvy friend Mark messaged me online. Completely out of the blue, he began asking about my ex-girlfriend.

"How often did you guys kiss?" he asked. "What's the farthest you've ever went with her?"

I slightly fabricated the truth about how much we kissed, but refused to answer anything else he posed. I told Mark it was none of his business. He tried to pry the information out of me by insistently repeating certain questions and resending messages that I hadn't replied to. I became annoyed with him and told him to leave it alone. He replied,

"Ok, I will. But I think you might have more interest in someone like…oh I don't know, Ricky Martin for example."

My heart absolutely sank. I'm sure I showed some type of guilt with my fumbling responses. I told him to shut up and tried to blow it off like it was nothing more than a mere joke. His proceeding sly responses and silence proved that he perhaps did know something. My worst fear came true. I couldn't stomach the effects it may have led to. I foresaw my life completely tumbling down around me.

I became absolutely consumed the entire night, and for days and weeks on end thereafter. I worried and wondered about whom he had told, and what would happen if my family and other friends found out. The thoughts ate away at me from the inside like a disease. They crippled me mentally and emotionally. I seriously contemplated suicide.

I felt completely betrayed by my friend and blackmailed. To a certain extent, he knew that he had some type of power over me for the remainder of our days at school. I went out of my way to remain nice to him. Not only were his actions of hacking into my computer cruel, they were illegal. By telling on him, I risked outing myself to the world. I couldn't do that. I instead placed high hopes on his intelligence level to know better than to brag about his illegal behavior to others.

I never trusted him again. I once considered Mark a good friend, and was close to his family as well. For the remainder of high school, this issue kept me up at night. Not college, not future jobs, but how long I could comfortably hide my secret, and how, if ever possible, I could still discover how to change myself to avoid the issue in its entirety. The mental drain and fear from the situation stopped me dead in my tracks from any thoughts I had to be myself. It pushed me even further into hiding. I battled depression alone.

High School Uncertainties

Throughout the last couple years in high school, I kept myself extremely busy. Less free time equated to less time to stress out about my sexuality. I joined the tennis and the crew teams. I took college level courses for credit, became the Vice President of National Honor Society, and directed a service program run at the junior high school. Heading into my senior year, I successfully campaigned for Class Presidency against the same girl that had been elected each year since the seventh grade.

Amidst all of my eclectic activities, athletics, and constant work at home for the family business, I had not the slightest idea of what I wanted to be when I grew up. I knew that I probably wouldn't be able to hide my secret forever. Because of such, I didn't have a clue what I could become as a professional one day. I could either screen myself forever and go after what I wished for, or come out of the closet and perhaps shoot myself in the foot.

I viewed gay people the same as society did: perverted, immoral and anti-religious people. There weren't visible gay role models or publicized pro-gay demonstrations or gatherings telling me anything different. I developed a pessimistic view for a happy and successful future, both personally and professionally. I went to bed so many evenings convinced that I would be alone forever, and thinking that I would be forced to hold on to this deep dark secret internally and eternally. I couldn't grasp the slightest idea of what it meant to live life as a gay male. The thought completely surpassed my comprehension.

Throughout the last year of high school my guidance counselors, teachers, and parents increasingly urged me to look at colleges. But the fact remained that I had not the slightest clue of what I wanted to do with my life. I really enjoyed mathematics and physics, so thought that I could get into teaching or perhaps engineering or architecture. How could I decide what I wanted to do with the rest of my life, when I couldn't even decide what to do with being gay?

With all of the confusion and pressures in high school, I worked up the courage to try and convince myself yet again that I could be straight. I tried my hardest to lie and filled my mind with images of women all day. I forced myself to check out good-looking women at school and at work. I once more put my sexuality and myself on trial, hoping the result would change.

Besides one fairly long relationship in middle school through the beginning of high school, I didn't have any other lasting relationships. While single, a girl Alyssa at school flirted on and off with me. It never seemed that serious. Alyssa was a pretty girl with a great sense of humor. As skinny as she was, she was very 'top heavy.' Most guys would have jumped at the chance to get with her. One day, she messaged me on AOL Instant Messenger. Our conversation started off as playful, until she became a bit more direct. She asked,

"How come you never gave me a chance to be your girlfriend?"

I didn't know what to say. I told her I was unsure of the reason, but that she was a very attractive girl.

"Well, would you ever kiss me?" she asked.

"I don't know?" I said. "Yes, I don't see why not."

"So you'd make out with me?"

"Yes, I would." I boldly and confidently responded.

"Prove it."

"Ok," I said. "Give me your address and I'll be right there."

My heart pounded not from excitement but from fear. I worked up a false sense of confidence, and told my parents that I was running over to a friend's house. I jumped in their Ford pickup truck. On the drive there, I spent half my time freaking out, as this was the last thing that I ever wanted to do. I spent the remainder convincing myself that I could in fact do it. I parked the truck and walked up to her doorstep. Panic shot through my body and took over. Thirty seconds passed. My brain convinced my right pointer finger to reach out and push the doorbell before giving in to the urge to flee. Alyssa opened the door. It opened right up to her living room. The TV was on, and the couch had pillows neatly propped up against one corner.

We conversed. I stalled as long as possible. After a few minutes of meaningless conversation, she raised her eyebrow at me.

"Well, are you going to prove what you said to me or what?"

I looked her in the eyes while trying to be as confident and non-awkward as possible.

"Of course I am," I said.

We kissed in the middle of the living room. She pulled me over towards the couch. She lay on the couch on her back against the stack of pillows and pulled me on top of her. We continued kissing for a few minutes. She pulled my hips tightly against hers. Nothing happened down there. I felt embarrassed that I couldn't even get slightly excited by this "passionate" moment. I didn't know what to do next. My mind raced and so did her hands. I felt absolutely nothing except wanting to get away from the situation as fast as I could.

A few minutes later, I heard a faint knock on the door. I jumped up from the couch like someone had just yelled "fire!" I ran to the door and peeked through the eyehole. Emily, one of our mutual friends from school stood at the door. I looked back at Alyssa lying on the couch. She suggested leaving Emily out there, and to pretend that nobody was home.

I swung the door open like there was a million dollars waiting for me on the other side. I welcomed Emily inside, and she asked how we were doing. I took note of Alyssa's face from across the room, which portrayed a vibe of annoyance by the disturbance. Emily asked, "Do you want me to come back later?" Before she even finished the sentence I jumped in, "No! By all means come on in, we're just hanging out and wouldn't want to be rude."

The three of us watched some TV and chatted for a bit about school. A few minutes later, I excused myself claiming that I had to get back to work. Back in the truck, I let out a huge sigh of relief. I couldn't help but to find the situation somewhat comical. I laughed, rolled my eyes in disbelief, gasped at what just happened, and hit myself upside the head the whole way home. It felt good to know that I wasn't crazy. This wasn't me, and this wasn't a choice that I could make. I had forced myself to temporarily make the choice to be "normal," to be straight, and it was one of the most uncomfortable and awkward lies that I had ever placed myself in. I thanked God for that perfectly timed knock on the door.

Preparing for College

In high school, I had friends that knew exactly what they wanted to do with their futures. They set themselves up for success since day one. I never fully pieced together the puzzle of school and all of its potential future impacts, or why I was even there in the first place. I worked hard to maintain good grades, but had more interest in skipping my study halls to play sports in the gym.

The last year of high school just flew by. I didn't prioritize college preparation, and postponed it until the last minute possible. My family and my guidance counselor continued to shed light upon why college should become my top priority. I took those tests to see what I wanted to do when I grew up. All of my interests aligned with either sports or math and physics. I narrowed my eventual college search down to about three to four schools, all with strong mathematics and engineering programs.

Despite the fact that I had grown up around multiple family businesses and worked at one since a very young age, I didn't consider schools with a good reputation for business. I watched my parent's business grow from a tiny startup to one of the landmark businesses in our town, continually growing in both size and popularity. I learned budgeting, profit margins, investments, marketing, contracting, and management. I didn't want to study business for four more years at college. For me, business was synonymous with all of what I already knew. It meant being constantly on-call for work while sitting at home and trying to relax after a long shift.

I became set on my choice of colleges and universities. I had no other idea what to do. They were all within an hour of my home, which was also important to me (my Mom's homemade Italian cooking kept me close). Compounded by a shrinking deadline for college applications, I quickly found myself behind on the whole process. Most of my friends had already sent about five or six applications to different schools and anxiously waited to hear news. I still had yet to visit a school, let alone apply to one. My Grandpa Tony asked if I wanted to go check out one of my choice schools with him.

My Grandpa dreamed of seeing me go to college. He wanted to attend school as a kid but instead was put right to work at a young age. My great grandfather didn't let him to go school. He had to work and make money, and that was that. Grandpa Tony became a master shoemaker and material-worker, and repaired just about anything imaginable. He became well known in Schenectady for his unmatched expertise in the trade.

Growing up while working in this environment, I could have easily followed my family's trend, or looked to take over one of the businesses. But my family wanted more for me. They saw more in me. Even though I felt like a piece of driftwood in the ocean, they pushed me to go to college. My parents and grandparents worked extremely hard to make sure they provided a better life for their own kids than they had themselves.

I hit the road with my Grandpa to visit my first ever college campus. We attempted to drive to one of my for sure schools of choice. On the way, we ran into a roadblock and a detour, and another, and then a closed-off bridge being fixed on one of the alternate routes. When we ran into a broken water pipe that closed another road, it seemed literally impossible to get to this University.

We stopped for a bite to eat and my Grandpa suggested, "Why don't we go check out another school, Siena College, right down the road?" I confidently reiterated which schools I wanted to attend, but I reluctantly obliged out of respect for my Grandpa's wishes. As we pulled into the campus, we were greeted with impressive brick buildings surrounded by beautiful landscaping. Siena's campus was gorgeous, and we easily navigated it by foot due to its intimidate size. After returning home and sharing my excitement with my parents, we immediately signed up for an official tour.

When I returned to campus for the tour, things only got better. Everything just seemed to fit. It took all of 30 minutes of walking around the campus to know that this was the place for me. I fell in love with the small class sizes, the beauty of the campus, and the impressive 17 NCAA Division 1 Sports the school boasted. My decision to apply became one of the easiest decisions of my life, which was in direct contrast to my normal compulsive indecisiveness.

I continued to visit colleges and Universities across New York State. Even after checking out other schools, I knew that Siena was the place for me, and the school I wanted to call home for the next four years of my life. I geared all of my efforts upon gaining admission to Siena.

During Christmas 2002, my parents left the room to retrieve one final present. I unwrapped a framed letter of acceptance from Siena College. I was in! Along with every important decision and event in my life, my family was front and center to experience it with me. Everything I had done in high school made sense in that moment. I anxiously looked forward to the future.

Lying in bed that evening, my temporary high of excitement slightly wore off. A certain degree of fear set in. I became anxious at the thought of living away from my parents for the first time in my life, and nervous to attend a big new school where I barely knew anyone. Most of all, it intimidated me to face college being gay without a soul in the world to talk about it with. I thought high school was tough with all the judgmental words I heard. I figured college would be the same or even worse yet. Movies depicted college as a place where people all drank and got crazy. If people knew about me in this type of atmosphere, I feared to be at the receiving end of some pretty cruel jokes.

In the back of my mind lurked the never-ending thought that one day I would eventually need to come out. However, I figured it would be completely unneeded and unnecessary to start off the next four years of my life as, "Hi, I'm Adam, and I'm gay." I figured if

people I met weren't putting forth, "Hi, I'm Abby, and I'm straight."
– then why should I have to put it out there? I felt so much more
than just that as a person. I didn't want to be defined solely because
of my sexuality.

Finding Christianity

As a child, I went to a Roman Catholic Church, but never really understand what it truly meant. I didn't care for church much and quite frankly I found it flat out boring. I knew that the Bible existed, and I knew we had to open it up for certain readings or to sing certain songs. Although my parents never pushed religion in my face as a kid, I knew that I would eventually be confirmed. Before my confirmation, I never opened up a Bible to read on my own other than while in class.

During my senior year, a kid named Nate came to our family's business looking for a job. My Mom hired him on the spot. Nate and I worked at the go-karts together and in the snack bar as well. We got along right away as our friendship revolved around sports and laughter. Nate asked me if I would come to his Lutheran church with him. After asking some questions about the Lutheran side of Christianity, I agreed to give it a shot.

Kids my age filled the church. We hung out and engaged in activities and conversation. I grabbed a few mini donuts and a bagel and selected my seat. The lively music from a small band filled the air. People clapped their hands and sang along. The sermon spoke to me. I found its meaning applicable to my life more so than those I heard in the Catholic Church. I attended church with Nate for the next few weekends. My faith and belief in God continued to grow stronger as I started to understand a little more of what the Bible and Christianity was all about.

I read through the entire book of Genesis. I enjoyed the two different stories of creation and analyzed them with Nate. I formed an understanding that both creation stories attempted by means of poetry to show the importance that God created us out of love. They didn't argue with one another. I came to understand that I couldn't read a passage in the Bible and take it literally without studying the entire context of that particular passage.

Previously, I focused too much on the "this vs. that" in order to find a definitive answer. However, I quickly realized that the Bible wasn't meant for its facts and stories to be solely interpreted in their literal words as written. Rather, the Bible provides stories about love and inspiration, about the promises of God's love for us, about the rules and manners we should treat another with, and how we should love everyone as Jesus did, unconditionally.

Nate gifted me a Bible. We successfully completed a reading challenge with one another and read through the entire New Testament. The four gospels captivated me. I learned all about Jesus' life and the lessons that He left us with. Nate and I continued going to church each week, and attended various retreats and some Sunday school classes together too. My curiosity and intrigue for Christianity grew hand-in-hand with my faith.

I believed in God as a child, but never before had I directly acknowledged God's presence in my life. Through my journey, I firmly came to believe that God really does exist. Previously, I imagined God as completely intangible, never showing His face. That summer however, I realized that God presented Himself to me through both the people and the situations that surrounded me.

UBUNTU and the Winds of Change

Nate and I traveled to Atlanta, Georgia as part of the Evangelical Lutheran Church of America (ELCA) national youth gathering. The gathering's theme was "UBUNTU" – described as "I am because we are, we are because Christ is." We celebrated our differences and learned and grew with the more than 20,000 youth from various churches across the country. I met many other teens that had similar beliefs as me, and we shared in constant fellowship.

For five days, our group and all other youth met in Atlanta's massive Georgia Dome. We experienced various speakers on the future of the ELCA, sermons from some of the nation's top Pastors, and took part in interactive songs, games, and dances daily. I experienced the Holy Spirit that week like never before. In one of the workshops, we painted our unique life's journey on a large cross. The activity allowed me to dig deep into my past accomplishments, regrets, and fears. I tried my best to symbolically represent them all through art. I felt the presence of God guiding me through my life's reflection and projection onto the cross with the stroke of each paintbrush.

On the last day of the event, our church group attended a final conference with Pastors and church leaders from across the country. Hundreds of people filled the conference room. They discussed various issues as related to the present and future state of

the ELCA. One of the "hot issues" on topic was homosexuality.
The proponent was an older gentleman who gently addressed the
topic. He advocated for the acceptance of homosexuality within the
church to the audience. A young spitfire lady followed him and
presented a much lengthier argument in opposition. She tried to
convince the audience that homosexuality was a mere decision that
could be changed. Her words absolutely infuriated me. The more
she continued on with her seemingly convincing arguments and
confident persona, the more I cringed.

As the debate opened up to the floor, Pastors and various
leaders in the room posed their questions to both speakers. The
audience posed watered-down and politically correct questions. My
entire table murmured in accordance with my internal level of
disagreement as she continued to speak. As the conversation
progressed, it became clear that she was winning the debate. She did
a better job outlining her case and coming across in a more self-
assured manner than the gentleman. The room swayed towards her
argument.

I reached my boiling point and couldn't take it anymore. I
had to say something. My mind raced a million miles an hour. I
debated if this was my coming out moment, revealing that I was gay
not only in front of a group of my close friends and Pastors, but a
conference room full of strangers and church leaders. I decided that
would be extremely too much. However, I knew of a girl in my high
school that was a lesbian.

I took in a slow, deep breath. My hands shook and my heart pounded in my throat. I forced myself to get over my nerves quickly. I shot my hand up passionately to ensure that I grabbed the speaker's attention. I stood up and introduced myself to the room.

"Excuse me ma'am," I said. "If you wouldn't mind, I would like to address one particular point that you have seemed to so overly suggest, that homosexuality is a 'decision,' a conscious choice. Out of curiosity, at what age specifically do you remember choosing to like men?"

She paused and slightly shook her head. I continued, "When did you personally and consciously choose to like, let's say, men over women?"

She appeared a bit flustered. I pressed on.

"A girl in my school classifies herself as a lesbian. To some of us it seemed strange at first that she liked girls. After all, she is a girl herself, why would she *choose* to like girls, right? Well, she insisted that she didn't 'choose' this; it just is the way that she is. For the very same reason that you cannot defend to me why you like men, she cannot 'defend' why she likes women, as it is simply the way that she was created. Imagine someone telling you that you had to begin to start liking women. Would you be able to change and convince yourself that you no longer liked men?"

"No, I don't think that I could," she replied.

"Exactly. It's no different for someone who identifies himself or herself as a homosexual. When you imply that homosexuals have the freedom of choice, then I challenge you to

46

turn the tables. What if someone told you, that you had to like women, because liking men was no longer acceptable? As funny as this may sound, this is what it feels like for a gay person to be told to switch their natural feelings of attraction. I believe I speak for a younger generation that is willing to come out and defend gay people – the very people whom you so declare as 'sinners' today, were still created in God's image. Thank you."

I sat down as calmly as possible, although my knees shook like crazy and I felt completely nauseous. Although unbeknownst to those around me, these were actually my feelings, my emotions, and my beliefs that I put out for the world to hear. Some of the audience applauded, mostly the younger people in the room, but some Pastors joined in as well. The conversation remained largely secular, so I held my own pretty well moving forward.

After the conference concluded, Pastors and leaders were encouraged to remain in the room to interact and network with one another. A couple of Pastors stopped me as our group made our exit.

"Hey! Can we talk with you for a quick minute?" they asked.

"Uh-oh. What could this be about?" I thought to myself.

"Yes...?" I hesitantly replied.

"We just wanted to say how refreshing it was to hear a youth speak up at an event like that. In particular, the story of the girl in your school. It was an interesting viewpoint that we have never been exposed to. Could you tell us a bit more about her?"

I talked about "her" even though I continued to describe myself. I felt like screaming, "It's me, it's me!" to them. I just about wanted to jump out of my skin and show them that a "normal" guy and person like me was gay. I discussed a few other issues, and they genuinely listened to what I had to say. It meant a big deal to me. I slept soundly that evening at the thoughts of progress, and dreamt of a day that gay people would be accepted within the church and within Christianity.

Lake Chautauqua Lutheran Center

In the summer between high school and college, Nate and I travelled five hours west to a place called Lake Chautauqua Lutheran Center (LCLC). This Christian camp hosted various campers and students all summer long, and we attended with some of our friends for Senior High Week. More than a dozen cabins were scattered around its large campus. It boasted multiple athletic fields, a sailing program right on the shoreline of the massive lake, and trails all around its acreage.

Our camp counselors hosted various devotional activities throughout the week. Mercy Me's "I Can Only Imagine" is one of my all-time favorite Christian songs, so when I saw a prayer workshop based around it, I immediately signed up. We reflected upon the song and listened to it several times. A counselor instructed us through sign language. We learned motions and signs that symbolized the song's lyrics. Utilizing a new method of communication allowed me to reflect upon the song's true meaning while applying it to my life. It also taught me a new and unique way to worship God.

As a cabin, we had our cabin rituals such as pegging each other with any object we could get our hands on before bed (it's a guy thing), to camp-wide rituals including ultimate Frisbee games and outdoor challenge courses. Each night, we sat around a massive fire pit and learned new worship songs. Our talented counselors gently strummed upon their guitars and led us through the music. Near the end of the week, we experienced one of the most memorable moments at LCLC together. Our counselors walked us through a "Christ Hike."

The staff members led us all around our camp's many small hills, throughout the woods, and eventually to the beautiful Chautauqua Lake. The leaders were incredibly and wholeheartedly into their character roles. Our journey began with the disciple John standing about 50 feet out in the lake. We witnessed him baptizing Jesus in front of a picturesque sunset across the lake. As Jesus began to make his way out of the water, John instructed us, "He is the Christ! Follow Him!"

We followed Jesus, and soon ran into a blind man. Jesus healed his vision. The man ran away and proclaimed thanks to God. Two Pharisees that doubted Christ began to call Jesus names. They continued to make fun of Him as we followed Jesus through the paths inside of the woods. Jesus interacted with the disciples Mathew and Judas. As he spoke with them, the Pharisees continued to verbally bash Jesus. They really got on my nerves. After a few more eventful scenes in Jesus' life, we then came to the scene where he was to be sentenced to death.

The head of the Roman Empire, Pontius Pilate, reluctantly gave the people what they wanted: the crucifixion and death of Jesus. As we observed this sentence, we were led to where Jesus would be killed. The Pharisees intertwined within our group. They shouted, "Yeah! Kill him!" and, "Give him what he deserves!" One word in particular brought me silently to tears. As the Pharisees continued to mock and yell names at Jesus, one of the women uttered under her breath the word "liar." Unlike all of the other words shouted, this word, this mumbled accusation of Jesus being a liar deeply bothered me. It made me feel like I called Jesus a liar through my disbelief in Him that he could love me for who I truly was, a gay Christian.

Like a monster lurking in the darkness, my fears and self-doubt inevitably crept back into my mind. I felt confused and didn't fully understand how I could in fact identify a both a gay male and a Christian. Was I truly even allowed to call myself both? I tried to convince myself that it was acceptable, but at times it seemed as strange to me as it was to the many disapproving voices from society. I unsuccessfully searched for a place within my heart to believe that God truly loved me for me.

On the last evening of camp, we had a large gathering in the main dining area of camp. We said our final goodbyes and thanked everyone for the incredible week we experienced. We gave out personalized "paper plate awards" in an awards ceremony to our counselors and various campers. Before the night ended, Tammy, a camp counselor from Australia approached me.

"I know that I recently just met you, and I know that this may come off as a bit strange," she said, "but I really feel like God is asking me to tell you something. I feel that I'm supposed to give you a message."

As one of the nicest and most respected counselors at camp, I trusted her personality and interactions with me as genuine. My ears perked up with intrigue.

"Adam, many girls are going to like you, and have liked you. But I feel that God wants me to tell you that one day, He has the right person for you. Be patient, love and trust in God, and you will find happiness one day with someone made just for you."

I became absolutely speechless. Nobody in my entire life ever told me that they felt as if God instructed them to give me a message, that in it of itself amazed me. If she said the word "girl" in place of the word "person" I would've disregarded her statement faster than a New York minute. But, she distinctly used the word *person*. I never before felt the realness of God like I did in that short conversation with Tammy. I held onto this statement during some of my toughest times that I faced in the years to come, amidst my loneliness and disbelief that I could ever find happiness.

Freshman Year at Siena

With all of my excitement, anxiety, and hopes and fears along for the ride, I began my career at Siena College. My roommate and I shared some of the same hobbies. He didn't drink or like to party much either, and our two good friends across the hall were the same. We made our own trouble, but at least none of us ended up getting an IV due to alcohol poisoning, which I witnessed on multiple occasions.

We routinely stayed up until 3:00-4:00am playing games in the hall like full-contact football, even though the walls were brick and the floors were concrete. I don't know how no one ever ended up in the hospital. We lived next to a group of baseball players. I never had experienced that much testosterone in one small area before. We learned to keep our fans on during the evening hours for white noise because they brought over girls just about every night. Their antics were ongoing like ours, except theirs were sexually fueled and usually mixed with a lot of alcohol.

On one evening, one of the muscular baseball players came over to our room wearing nothing but a white sock on his package. He casually sauntered in our dorm room while my friends and I did our homework and listened to music. His other teammates cracked up behind him. We yelled at him to get out, while his buddies egged him on. Amidst all of the commotion, I found myself quickly glancing down at that white sock, almost involuntarily. He saw me and yelled, "Mastroianni, did you just look at my thing?"

Everyone became temporarily quiet and looked over at me. I turned it back on him and immediately fired back, "You're the idiot that's walking around with nothing but a sock on your dick, what do you expect?!"

Everybody laughed, including him, and they made their way back to their rooms. I sighed and let out a deep breath. I gladly returned back inside of my all too comfortable and safe 'closet.' The interaction made me want to slam the door and bolt the lock on it, too.

I set myself up with a strong math and physics curriculum freshman year. I didn't initially declare a major, as Siena didn't have an established engineering or architectural major. While pushing through various physics and calculus courses, I seriously questioned if either would be the right major for me. Was I leaning towards becoming a math or physics teacher? What would I do if I didn't want to teach? Teaching seemed like a good fit, but I didn't want to limit myself. I felt enclosed my freshman year, and that there was more for me to explore and discover. I needed to expose myself to new activities, clubs and interests, and find out what else the world had to offer.

Although I'm a white male, I always related to minorities, and they likewise had to me. Even though I wasn't yet out as a minority, I knew deep within myself that I certainly was one in my own regard. During the year, my friend groups expanded and I tried new things. My friends encouraged me to join the Black and Latino Student Union and the Asian Student Association (ASA). The clubs were great. They were so open, so free and accepting, and I learned a lot in regards to what was important to them as minority groups. I wanted to join the Gay and Straight Alliance, but I feared the risk of giving myself away. I didn't want to openly give people a reason to think twice about my sexuality.

Through the ASA, I found out about a dance team known as Siena College Bhangra. I never heard of Bhangra before, but discovered that this little white boy was made for it. Bhangra is a traditional Indian dance originating from the Punjab region of India. Modern day Bhangra evolved to include many traditional Punjabi dance moves fused with current dance styles including hip-hop. After watching a performance of our college's team, I became completely moved by the music and inspired to join.

I inquired about joining the team and thought I could just sign up to participate. I couldn't have been more wrong. For a week straight, members of the team taught me and a group of 15 others a detailed choreography. The music and beat structure were completely new to me, as were all of the fast movements that required constant jumping and keeping rhythm with my entire body. Not only did we have to learn the choreography for dance elements, we learned constant formation changes as well. I did my best to learn the routine and practiced for hours even after the official practices concluded.

At the end of the week, a panel of senior team members judged us one by one as we completed the routine. With each note they jotted down and glance they gave one another, I became increasingly nervous. I received a few looks that insinuated, "Hmmm…white boy, why are you here?" I finished out my routine. The team embraced me when I showed them my rhythm and threw in a few back flips as well. A week or so later, I found out that I made the team. We practiced for two to three hours every night while training for regional and national competitions.

I also vowed for a spot on Siena's NCAA Division 1 Men's Tennis Team. Although I only had two years of tennis experience under my belt in high school, I was driven to continue my athletics career in college. I competed against most guys who played and trained their entire lives, and some who were recruited or on scholarship to play. I didn't have the benefit of years of coaching or training, but had a gift of picking up things extremely quickly. Having watched tennis for years, I did my best to replicate what my favorite players like Andre Agassi, Roger Federer, and Venus Williams did. After winning a few crucial matches, I successfully landed one of the spots on our team.

I learned the meaning of true organization in a hurry. I had double practices for tennis (weights in the morning and cardio in the evenings), and Bhangra practice each night. I also joined the campus's Catholic Church choir. I completed my academic work with whatever free time remained. I routinely stepped outside of my comfort zone during my freshman year and pushed myself to new limits. Keeping so busy at school allowed for a diverse and rapid growth of my self-discovery process. I began to express myself more freely, with the strict exception of my sexuality.

Taking a Risk

On the verge of my 20th birthday during my sophomore year, I woke up and knew that I had to be myself or else I was just going to burst. I must tell someone, anyone, and stop thinking about what I said or did or how I acted or felt. Going to school right outside of Albany, NY, I was a three-hour drive from Boston. I thought, "Why not go?" to one of America's friendliest gay cities. I visited Boston a few times as a child for field trips in school, and once or twice with my family. I had yet to visit Boston as an independent adult. I decided to go to my first ever gay club.

I drove to an out of town Barnes and Nobles and read the Boston City Guide. I looked up gay and lesbian nightclubs, and wrote down their addresses and information for future reference. I checked my Facebook page to see if I had any immediate friends or family members that may recognize me or my vehicle in that part of town. I made up my mind to go on the following Saturday night, and picked one of the larger clubs in town to attend. The week moved at a snail's pace, but finally and inevitably, Saturday arrived.

For the first time in my life I needed a fake ID. I asked one of my friends to do it for me. She willingly obliged, but with a puzzled face as she knew I didn't drink or go out to bars. I told my college friends I was heading out with some other friends and hit the road, Boston bound. I took the automated tollbooth reader off of my vehicle for the highways. I left no chance for a trace of my travels, and paid the tolls in cash only.

I felt liberated when I got behind the wheel. I never before allowed myself to experience the feeling of genuine independence, due to my constantly inhibited expressions and emotions. For the entire ride, my heart raced and beat out of my chest. My fingers clenched the steering wheel and I drove extra carefully as I had no alibi if I got into an accident. I turned on the heat. I got hot, and then turned on the A/C. I got cold, and switched back to heat. I couldn't find a temperature to satisfy my excessive jitters. After this back and forth game, and three of the longest hours, I finally pulled up to the club.

I peered into a few windows that faced the street. Unable to catch a glimpse inside, I made one more pass and inspected the crowd. I parked. I couldn't move, and my hand wouldn't reach down to undo my seatbelt. I looked forward to this all week, but I couldn't even get out of the car. I worried about the fake ID I carried. I could have easily just wasted a three-hour drive each way if I got turned away at the door. My nerves ran at such great speeds. Was I betraying my parents? Would my friends treat me as an outcast if they knew who I really was? What if I ran into someone that I knew? The questions piled up, and twenty minutes went by in the car. I put the key back in the ignition to drive back to Albany. After a deep breath I declared out loud, "You're doing this!"

I made a lap around the block of the club while trying to get my nerves out, before finally stopping at its doors. The entrance was dimly lit and a bouncer stood right in front of me. I fumbled through my pocket to pull my ID from my wallet. It took all of my strength to play it cool. He stared down at my ID for a second, and I thought for sure he would question me. He looked up from my ID and said, "I just love that shirt!" I let out a huge gasp of air and said, "Thank you!" I quickly grabbed my ID and buried it deep within my pocket. I paid a small cover, and walked down a narrow stairway to find someone checking my stamped hand. I froze. My chest, arms, and legs trembled with nerves. The club was incredibly large and so many good-looking guys surrounded me. While in a deep stare, the employee at the bottom of the stairs, Lucas, said, "Are you alright?" I blinked and snapped out of it.

I talked with Lucas, and informed him that he was officially the first person I came out to. A little flamboyant, yet not overly, he opened his arms and gave me a big hug proclaiming, "Welcome home honey!" It put me slightly at ease as I let out some nervous laughter. I asked Lucas to share his story with me. I asked him endless questions about his coming out, his family, and everything else in between. Lucas shared that his family disowned him when he came out, and he lost almost all contact with them, back in Brazil. I became fascinated by everything he told me, from all of his life's struggles to the motivation he found in order to find his own unique journey. His want and his need to be his true self inspired me. I desperately wanted to get there eventually. For now, the thoughts and fears of social and family acceptance weighed much more heavily upon me than my desires to be comfortable in my own skin.

Hearing how his family disowned him further terrified me at the thought of coming out.

We chatted for nearly a half hour. He encouraged me to go dance, and to spend some time trying to meet someone. I told him I could never work up the nerves to go approach someone alone. Lucas then asked me who I thought was cute. I pointed at the shirtless guy dancing up a storm on the dance floor, with his toned physique and handsome features. As it happened, Lucas knew him, and called him over by name. With each step that he took towards us, my anxiety level increased. I stood quiet as Blake and Lucas began talking. Lucas introduced us. When Blake found out that it was my first time in a gay club he lit up, and he took me by the hand. He immediately led me to the dance floor. "Let loose man!" he said.

No other sense on my body seemed to work except the sense of touch on my right hand. I didn't see anyone else around me, even though I originally noticed the packed club. I didn't hear the pounding music that once seemed so deafening. For the first time in my life, I held a guy's hand. It felt so natural, and so right. We danced. My senses slowly kicked back in, and I danced in and out of the neon green strobe lights flashing around us. I felt the rhythm of the music. My hands waved to the heavy techno beats and my head shook from side to side. I closed my eyes and became entranced.

I noticed a missed a call from my Mom on my cell phone. She left me a voicemail. A few songs later, I went to the bathroom to check it. She invited me to church with she and my Dad the next morning. I had routinely made the short 30-minute drive home from college to do so. But after my long drive home later that night, I didn't want to get a measly few hours of sleep and then hit the road again. Guilt overtook me. If I called my Mom back, I would've lied on my whereabouts or why I couldn't make it the next morning. I broke down and cried in the bathroom stall. A couple of minutes passed. I regained my composure. I remind myself why I had gone there in the first place. I pushed aside my feelings of betrayal, and realized that I needed to be selfish in that moment. I needed to live it out for me and for nobody else, and for a chance at finding my own happiness.

Blake and I proceeded to dance and joke around on the dance floor. We hit it off. A few songs later, he leaned in and gave me a kiss. Time stopped. Sparks flew and fireworks thundered loudly in the background. My knees weakened and my mind fell into a daze. It felt incredible to kiss someone that I was actually attracted to and interested in. Every single other kiss before then had been with girls. I kissed girls because it's what guys do. However, I didn't need to fake or force this kiss. I knew from that very moment that I couldn't hide that part of me forever, because it felt like home. My body and mind said, "Adam, seriously, what is wrong with you, and what took so damn long?"

Before parting from the club later in the evening, Blake and I exchanged numbers. We stayed in touch sporadically throughout the following year or so. I shared with him my interest in writing a book and telling my story and that I had already begun doing so. He encouraged me to continue working upon it. I confided in Blake my utmost fears of eventually coming out one day, and learned more about his story as well. I found something that I didn't expect to find when I went to a club to go dancing, my first gay friendship. We kept in touch for a bit via phone and email, but with us living hours apart, we eventually lost touch.

As for Lucas, one month after we met, he reached out to me. His parents were tragically killed in a carjacking in Brazil. A theft wanted to steal his parent's car, and after they put up a struggle, they were shot dead on the spot. Completely distraught, he informed me that he would soon return home to be near his remaining family. My heart ached for him. I wasn't sure which was worse, losing his parents emotionally when he came out and fully losing touch with them, or now having lost them physically. They would never get the chance to get through this "issue" of him being gay. Sadly, after this conversation, I never heard from Lucas again. This news left me thinking on many different levels, and temporarily set me back on any courageous feelings of coming out in the near future. I realized the potential for disruption that I may cause within my family and friend circles, and upon my daily life.

A Non-Welcoming Bible Study

During the later half of my sophomore year, my cousin Jamie invited me to join her at a weekly college Bible study. "The people are young, fun, lively, and love Jesus!" she said. I gladly agreed to participate. Upon arrival, I found myself in the midst of a game of dodge ball. Jamie said, "Pick up a ball!" and we joined in the action. I launched multi-colored Styrofoam balls at a wall of strangers, and protected two of my new teammates from incoming shots. "Thanks, man! I'm Jeremy," one guy said. Lindsay, another one of my teammates, introduced herself as well. As the game concluded, my cousin picked up the last dodge ball and tossed it across the room. She wiped a small bead of sweat off of her forehead with her forearm. "Fun, huh?"

"Thanks for inviting me," I said. "But we actually study the Bible too, right?"

The group leader Chad let out a small laugh as he patted me on the back. "Good game, Adam." He said, as he pulled the drawstring up on the mesh sack and hauled the gear away. After a quick stop at the water fountain, I opened my Bible in the circle of 20 other college-age students. Chad began,

"I'd like us to open up to Paul's letter to the Romans."

I flipped my Bible open with my notebook in hand. We read through parts of the letter, and then Chad revealed the theme of the week's study.

"Tonight we will be discussing homosexuality in the Bible. We will be addressing specific verses that pertain to this topic and exploring their implications."

"Just perfect," I thought to myself.

I remained quiet and observed the group and my new surroundings. Chad selected two verses regarding homosexuality. He divorced them entirely from their context.

"As you can see," he said, "God shows us that homosexuality is a sin."

My eyes squinted and glanced around the room to gather a sense from the group. Slight head nods from the attendees quickly exhibited mutual agreement. Sweat formed on my upper forehead just under my hairline. My heart slowed down after the game concluded, but immediately sped back up due to the evening's topic. Chad finished his opening statements, and opened up to the group for discussion.

"Paul shows us that God condemns gay and lesbian people. They are not acceptable in the eyes of God." Jeremy shared.

"We need to pray for homosexuals stuck in their trap of sin." Lindsay confidently added.

The group unknowingly condemned me. One by one, they casted stones upon me. Part of me felt loved by God, but what if I was wrong? I revisited lifelong struggles as thoughts rushed through my head and contradicting messages filled my mind. The group discussed ways to pray for gay and lesbian people. Stereotypes were made surrounding LGBT lifestyles and their "choices." My frustrations silently grew. Chad posed a question to the group.

"How much or how little should we interact with homosexuals both in and outside of the church? For those of us who have gay friends, does it send them a bad message to lead them to believe that it's ok to be gay?"

"How can we isolate these verses," I said, leaning forward and raising my voice slightly, "from the overall context and significance of Paul's letter? Paul's letter focuses upon the message of love, faith, and hope that God provides us with. It doesn't merely isolate a group of people as outcasts in God's eyes. How can we apply a verse written 2,000 years ago that suggested abusive behaviors including rape, to encompass what we now refer to as homosexuality?"

Lindsay's left knee bounced up and down as she fidgeted with her pen upon her notebook. She impatiently bit her lower lip and waited for me to finish speaking. She jumped in.

"We cannot refute verses written in the Bible. Homosexuality is wrong as shown by these verses, and we cannot overlook or disregard Holy Scripture. We cannot make exceptions to the fact that God clearly shows us that being gay is a sin."

I replied, "We don't have to look much further to utilize your same argument against others. Paul's writings have been misused to suppress and judge every single group in history from Jews, women, black people, divorcees, mentally ill people, interracial marriages, and the list goes on. Paul's point to his letter is that we are all set aside from God, but through grace we're all loved and saved. Paul also strictly emphasized that nobody has the right to judge but God himself."

My cousin glared at me from across the circle. I shrugged my shoulders. I continued on, yet cautiously maneuvered my level of passion and interest as to not reveal myself as gay. Each student in the room disagreed with me, and remained steadfast in their anti-gay stance relating to Christianity. I stood alone in my sentiments. I had much to say, but I remained calm for the remainder of the study. Another "anti-gay" passage was then referenced. My patience and nerves ran thin. Outnumbered, I fell quiet and disengaged.

My eventual coming out would undoubtedly be faced with many opinions like this both in and outside of my family. I tried to disregard their statements, but couldn't help but to still hear their judgmental words. My high hopes for this Bible study group diminished. My all-too-familiar thoughts and fears of not being fully loved by God or by those around me resurfaced. Ironically, in my first attempt to come closer to God through a college-aged fellowship group, it temporarily drove me away from Christianity. I never returned there again.

Returning to LCLC

After my freshman year at college, I worked at LCLC over the summer as a camp counselor. I wanted to give back to kids what I so gratefully experienced as a camper the year prior. During my sophomore year at school, I happily accepted the full-time position again. The experience to work at another job excited me, as I worked solely for my family business since I was nine years old. As a Christian camp counselor I didn't make much money at all, but the opportunities exceeded the pay ten-fold. Being exhausted after staying up the night with little Timmy because he missed home or cleaning up after he wet the bed was just a part of the job. It didn't matter how many times I sang the same song or taught the same lesson. I got to help kids build their faith and learn about God.

Upon arrival, the beautiful Chautauqua Lake welcomed me back home for the summer. On the first day of camp orientation, the counselors were broken up into various groups to get to know one another better. Later in the day, we broke up into even smaller groups for what we referred to as "IP time" (interpersonal time). We discussed our lives and our individual journeys that brought us to LCLC. After we shared our ministry goals during the summer with one other, we discussed various controversial issues current in the church. We discussed women's roles in the church and the family, divorce, and various religions and their beliefs. We then discussed homosexuality.

I immediately recalled my previous encounter with this topic just a few short months ago. I tensed up. My co-counselor Toni opened up the discussion by sharing her point of view. She spoke with passion.

"I don't even know why we have to differentiate between homosexuals and heterosexuals. We're all God's children and there should be no difference."

I wanted to jump up and give Toni a hug, but I remained seated and quiet. Lewis then spoke up.

"This issue has deeply affected my family. Three years ago, my mom divorced my dad. She left him for another woman. She is a lesbian. My mom claims to have known this her whole life, but never had the courage to tell anyone. Dealing with the issue has been extremely difficult on my dad and us, but we have grown to love and accept my mom for who she is. I don't know if God loves her just the same, but I know that we have found it in our hearts to do so."

Lewis' story shocked me. I couldn't imagine being that far in the game of lies and being married and with kids, and then coming out. Hearing this story helped me realize what I did not want to do to another person, or people. However, it encouraged me to hear more stories about gay and lesbian people. It seemed that more and more people knew an LGBT person. My world and my familiar place of loneliness seemed a bit larger and more occupied than myself as its sole resident.

As the conversation ensued, the majority of responses affirmed a general approval or understanding of the issue at hand. Kellie was different though. She sat quietly with a wrinkled face to suggest her disapproval. Kellie voiced that her parents always told her that being gay was a sin. It troubled her to hear so many contrasting viewpoints. She began to ask questions to the group.

"How do you know that being gay is not a sin? Didn't God make man and woman so that they could reproduce? I have been raised to believe that God strictly forbids gay people into heaven. You guys think differently?"

Kellie was genuine with her inquiries. She willingly listened to viewpoints from the group. As Toni and Lewis spoke up and began to answer her questions, I noticed the tension slowly departing from Kellie's face. She may not have agreed with everything said, but she discussed the issue at hand rather than pretending that it didn't exist, or as if it was strictly a sin that demanded repentance. She respectively engaged in the conversation and I admired that about her. The discussion continued, but I found myself drifting off into a daydream. I thought,

"My generation will be in power one day. This must have been what the younger generations sounded like back when women didn't have the right to vote, or when slavery and segregation were still being upheld, or when the Civil Rights Movement took the nation by storm. Younger generations such as mine will shape our very country's future."

I realized that even though it might take some time, and hardships and setbacks will be faced along the way, my generation is unstoppable if our efforts combined to vocalize equality for gay people. It inspired me to hear young Christians stand up for LGBT people. It further inspired me to see Kellie be open to discussing the topic, even though it went against her upbringing.

Later in the week I got pulled aside by a visiting Pastor. Pastor Ruth had known me from the previous year, and approached me with an offer. She asked if I had ever considered seminary. At one point I had. I shared that I struggled with my call in life and didn't really feel called right now to do so. I politely thanked her and turned down the offer. She encouraged me to consider it, and offered me an all-expense paid trip out of state to attend a seminar. Pastor Ruth also shared that she once struggled with womanhood and her personal calling. As a younger woman, societal and religious beliefs wouldn't allow her to become a Pastor because of her gender.

I desperately wanted to ask her what she thought about the gay issue. However, I had never even heard about a gay or lesbian Pastor, and coming out to a religious figure as the first person in my immediate life didn't entice me. Comfortably, I bit my tongue and continued on with the conversation as if nothing bothered me.

I thought I could never become a gay Pastor. The issue puzzled me as much as it did the rest of society. The effects of a lifetime's worth of hearing stereotypes and bigotry regarding gay people truly affected me. It affected my own perception of what I could and could not do or accomplish in my life. As a 20-year old adult who had never smoked, drank, or had sex, I thought that if I became a Pastor or even a teacher, society would view me as nothing but an immoral pervert. Thoughts like those severely limited my aspirations regarding those and other careers.

The Dilemma Awaits

My second summer at LCLC flew by. The experience as a camp counselor proved just as meaningful, fun, and exhausting (in a good way) than the year prior. The most anticipated week of all summer remained, Senior High Week. We took off a full week beforehand to refresh and clear our minds. Most counselors stayed around camp, but I took the long train ride home to spend the time with my family.

Upon arrival, it only took a day or two to fall right back into the swing of things with my home life. My family and I got up and began work around 8:00am each day. We used a leaf blower to clean the golf course and property, calibrated the batting machines, fixed the go-karts and fueled them, cleaned the party rooms, and prepared the machines in the snack bar. We closed the business down around 10:00pm each night, preparing to repeat our routine the following day. From April to October, my family operated on this schedule. No nights, holidays, or weekends off. We referred to ourselves as "worms" because we only went out when it rained, sneaking out to a movie or a family dinner in between the raindrops.

My parents were long overdue for a needed break and outlet to relax after their 11th year in business. They purchased a small piece of property about an hour and a half from our home, sitting on a small lake in the Adirondacks. The property had beautiful mature trees surrounding it, mountains in plain sight, and a small cabin that overlooked the body of clear water. My Dad and I worked upon the land and cabin for two days during my visit home. We enjoyed completing projects together, and we set out to accomplish a lot in two days. We built a small deck, raised a floor level in the house, and painted the cabin's outside. We worked nonstop. Removed from my daily routines, I reminisced about my younger days and the simplicities of life.

As a kid my meals showed up three times a day, I hung out with friends constantly, and I got bedtime stories read to me just about every night. Stresses in my life included eating vegetables that I didn't like, or someone taking away my favorite toy. I didn't have work, bills to pay, or the need to budget for rent or a car payment. I never lost sleep over credit card worries or taxes of any kind. And, no matter how much fun I had with my friends or family, nothing ruined my day if I remembered that I was gay. That's exactly what happened on this day.

My Dad and I had a great final day at the campsite, grabbed some quick dinner, and hit the road to head home. We chatted and listened to some of our favorite music together, oldies from the 1950's and 1960's. But mentally just eating away at me from the inside, this thought and fear took complete hold over me. One day I needed to tell something that would result in me being looked at forever differently. The thoughts and fears ran rampant in my mind on this drive home, as they did on a daily basis. I couldn't imagine my name spread around as gay in my community, school, or within my friend networks. I pictured my extended family and lifelong family friends expressing their absolute disbelief and disapproval.

I became accustomed to facing each day with these same worries troubling me. Everything I did from waking up to hanging out with friends or family, to work, to school, and praying before bed, I had this issue on my mind. I loved my family so incredibly much, and the thought of disappointing them ripped out my heart. My paranoia of being judged and unaccepted shattered any bit of hope to come out with the truth. Like a black cloud looming over my head, these fears consumed my every thought. I felt like I was slowly dying on the inside.

Senior High Week

On the long train ride back to LCLC, I used most of the time to prepare for the upcoming Senior High Week at camp. I planned with a higher level of creativity and relevance for this high school aged group in mind. Because of the popularity of the week, not all counselors got a group of campers. When I arrived at camp, Nate and I got assigned to a cabin as co-counselors. We shouted with excitement and high-fived.

The following morning, campers began to arrive. More than 100 campers quickly filled up our large dining area and indoor center. Three of my previous campers, Brandon, Taylor, and James ran up to me from across the room.

"Adam! I earned all A's and two B's at school this past year!" Brandon proclaimed. He then pointed down at a string tied around his ankle. He looked at me and smiled.

Before departing from camp the previous year, I had my campers sit in a circle and wrapped a string around our left ankles. It interconnected us all. I closed the activity in a prayer, and cut the string, tying if off upon each of our ankles. I told my boys the lessons of God, teamwork, and friendship didn't end here. I told them whenever they got overwhelmed or stressed at school or in life, to look down upon their ankle and remember the brotherhood they had at camp and the support they have in one another and in God.

My string had survived the year too. I smiled at Brandon, and showed him my ankle. Taylor and James excitedly did the same thing. We gathered like a group of reunited family members. Cabin assignments were distributed. I luckily had two of them in my cabin again this year. Nate and I took our group of eight campers to the athletic fields and let them burn off some energy. We headed back to our cabin and walked our campers through cabin and camp rules, and outlined the upcoming week's activities.

On our first evening together, we had them write down their expectations and doubts about camp, along with their biggest fears and past mistakes. We stuffed the papers into glass bottles. We took them down to a large fire pit with their bottles in hand. One by one, the kids smashed them into the fire. We talked about freeing our minds and allowing ourselves to completely surpass our expectations of camp. We challenged them to symbolically let go of their past mistakes and fears by watching them be destroyed by the fire.

We all sat around the fire on large stumps that had been repurposed into seats. Although some familiar faces and campers surrounded me, my cabin this year had one noticeable difference. I had a very flamboyant gay camper, Sam. In the midst of our group discussion, Sam began to cry. I lead my campers through the topic of acceptance during our first night together, and worked upon my own personal acceptance of both him, and ironically of myself as well. With my closeted feelings to the issue of homosexuality aside, I walked the line of objectivity and opened the topic for discussion.

For a few seconds, silence took over the group. James started to push around some dirt with a large stick he had picked up along our walk, and then looked up towards the fire. The bright fire illuminated his face in an orange hue against the dark night's backdrop. He looked around at his fellow campers and said,

"We're all created equally in the eyes of God, Sam."

I let the group take the statement in.

"Yes," another camper shared, "Sam, it doesn't matter if you're gay. To us, we're all brothers and we're all in this week together. We won't treat you any differently."

My senses heightened. The smell of the fire became prominent. The stars above me on the cloudless night shined vividly. I heard each and every crackle from the logs in the fire. I glanced around the circle and analyzed everyone's micro expressions and body language. Sam remained emotional. James then got up, and walked towards Sam. He bent down, and gave Sam a hug.

"It's all good," James told him.

One by one, my campers all got up and hugged Sam. I choked up watching them all embrace him. Brandon shared,

"If anybody messes with you this week, they've got all of us to answer to!"

I sat back and observed as the conversation continued. My campers seemed farther along in their personal acceptance of homosexuality than me, and I was the gay one. The conversation set the tone for the rest of the week. Nate and I learned from them as much as they did from us. As the week progressed, Sam fit in to each day's activities, and each night's discussions as his genuine self. The kids kept up their promises.

Throughout the week, one kid in the group proved a challenge. Cole always found a way to cause trouble, and started fights with kids verbally and even physically at times. He shared very little in group or individual settings, and rarely had anything polite to say when he did speak up. He also seemed over the whole religion issue. One night our group travelled to a large field. We spread out to let our campers sit and reflect upon whatever they wanted. A blanket of stars covered the sky. Cole got his hands on a flashlight, and shined it in everyone's eyes. I walked over to him to scold him for bothering others. Frustrated at my failed attempts to get through to Cole for days, I switched it up. I decided not to discipline him, and pretended that it didn't happen. I sat next to him on the grass.

"What are you thinking about?" I asked him.

He put the flashlight down and leaned back. I followed suit, and lay down in the cool grass with my eyes facing up towards the sky.

"I think I found a way to see and understand God."

Stunned, I proclaimed,

"Really! And how is that?"

"If you look up at the stars it's almost like God is directly communicating with us. If you look closely, He is showing us shapes through the stars. A little while ago I saw a huge smiley face looking down on me. It had two really bright stars for eyes, and dimmer ones for the mouth."

Talking about God with Cole was the last thing I ever imagined coming out of this conversation. We proceeded to talk about faith and his life. I provided him a full chance to speak his mind. We discussed respect and nonviolence, and he voiced his acknowledgement. I noticed some heat lightning in the distance and a few clouds rolling in. We all walked back to our cabin, with Cole and I behind the group to continue our conversation. We came to a point about 100 yards away from our cabin. Cole stopped.

"I've noticed that if you watch the lightning, it's almost as if God is telling us where to go," he said. "If you look closely, you'll notice it's only above our cabin."

I looked up as a huge flash of light awoke the sky directly above our cabin. Two more flashes quickly followed. Clouds had separated just enough above our cabin in the sky as if to create a window to view the lightning.

"You see," Cole said, while pointing towards the sky, "out of the entire sky all around us, lighting is only flashing above our cabin. It's almost like God is calling us home."

As the flashes continued in the same spot for the remainder of our walk, I noticed that the rest of the sky remained covered in darkness. Cole quietly finished walking home with the rest of the group, and didn't make one single peep or stir of trouble for the remainder of the night. He sat peacefully in the cabin and kept to himself. I got chills down my spine, amazed to see someone experience God, maybe even for the first time.

When it came time for our goodbyes later in the week, Nate and I stood on the porch of our cabin. Our kids all came up to us one by one when their parents arrived to pick them up. We reminisced about our outdoor challenge courses, days spent on the lake, and impromptu food fights. They thanked us. Every single one of our campers cried as they hugged us and said their goodbyes. As much as I tried not to cry, they definitely got some tears out of me that day. I felt like an older brother or parent to them all. After two summers of this routine, I decided that this would be my last year as a camp counselor.

Junior Year: Changing Course

My upcoming junior year promised excitement. I roomed with two of my best friends on the tennis team. Doing so proved extremely beneficial, especially during the beginning of the season with hectic practice schedules. However, I realized that as a college junior I no longer had the luxury of time on my side. I remembered the first day of my freshmen year in college, and even the first day of my freshmen year in high school. They seemed like yesterday. I approached my junior year differently. Up to that point in life, I just went through the motions and worked hard in school to check off all the boxes. I never fully understood or grasped what all of my work signified, or how it would forever impact my future path. I needed to buckle down academically.

My grades remained steady in math and physics, but my future remained uncertain. My work as a substitute high school teacher persuaded me not to pursue teaching at the moment. I made the difficult decision to forgo this career path, and start something anew. I continued pushing the idea of business away, but realized that perhaps business called and chased me, not the other way around. My experiences and maturity in the business world at such a young age provided me with a unique competence, which I owed directly to my parents.

As a liberal arts school, Siena had diverse requirements for any major. I took a business class to satisfy a requirement in my junior year. I wanted to get an "A" and check off the requirement. Then I met Professor Deborah Kelly. Professor Kelly changed my mind, my major, and my outlook on the future. I had less than two years left to complete my four-year college degree, and I didn't even know which subject to choose. Professor Kelly brought up the business major as a viable option, since I had already satisfied a few requirements in other areas. I voiced my concerns about business, and how I wanted nothing to do with it.

Professor Kelly mapped out a plan of action and how I could still graduate on time. She reviewed the endless possibilities of the industry. We researched and reviewed the diverse companies and opportunities that existed. After thoughtful consideration, and a few long nights spent pondering the possibility, I went for it. Off went my journey into overloading coursework during the last two years of my college days. I signed up for summer courses as well, to ensure that I graduated on time.

Amidst my jam-packed athletic, academic, and extracurricular schedules, my junior year became the best college year yet. I formed some of the closest friendships of my life. Most importantly, I did something that I didn't know I was ready to do yet. With my expanding and maturing mind, my ever-growing voice from within refused to remain silent. I finally worked up the courage to tell the first friend and first person close to me the deepest secret of my life.

A Breath Of Freedom

I suspected that my friend Alex at school was gay. He seemed like me, completely closeted. I felt extremely comfortable talking with Alex, and thought I could open up to him about the top secret matter. Just a short while into my junior year, the timing seemed right. I desired more than ever before to bring the topic to discussion. For a couple of days, I waited for the exact opportune time.

I couldn't stop thinking about finally telling someone about me, everything about me. I felt as if I had a bright light shining from within me that I could no longer contain in its forced darkness. I had to let it out. One evening, I ran into Alex at the dorm. My body and facial expressions exhibited nerves and anxiousness. We stepped into my dorm room to chat. My muscles tightened and my palms grew sweaty. I couldn't look him in the eyes.

"Is everything alright?" he asked.

His concerned face attempted to elicit information from me. I tried to start off the conversation confidently.

"I…" then I stopped.

"Well, I…" I paused again. I smiled and laughed awkwardly for a brief second and looked the other way. I realized the magnitude of difficulty behind finally uttering the words. I held them captive for so many years and my initial instincts wanted to keep them guarded. I rubbed my hands back and forth upon my knees. I questioned my own decision-making process. My eyes looked across the floor in front of me, still avoiding direct eye contact. Alex remained quietly seated across the room.

"I just need a few minutes," I said. "To clear my mind and find the right words to say what I need to."

Images flashed through my mind from childhood to adulthood. I thought about my family. I thought about my friends. I revisited lifelong struggles that led me to question if I would ever be looked at the same again. I finally said,

"You know, sometimes it's just really hard to feel like a normal person."

"What do you mean? When? Any examples...?" he asked.

I fell speechless again. I couldn't figure out how to approach it. It seemed nearly impossible to proclaim the words out loud to someone in my immediate life. I grabbed a picture from my wall and handed it to him. He threw his hands up and said, "And?" I pointed at the various guys in the picture, and gave him an insinuating look with overly expressive eyes. He leaned back in his chair. He appeared to somewhat catch my drift, but refused to voice the words that I so desperately searched for. He wanted me to come to terms with myself on my own time, in my own words.

I had one of my favorite Christian CDs playing in the background of my dorm room. I thought to myself, "God, if it's the right time for me to tell him now, then let my favorite song from the CD play next." The CD contained around 15 songs, and while on shuffle, that song came on next. Though perhaps just a mere coincidence, it pushed me over the edge and helped me make up my mind. I grabbed a piece of paper and a pen out of my desk drawer. I wrote, "I like him" on the note. I underlined the word 'like' twice.

"Wait, so do you just like him?" Alex asked, "Or do you like all H-I-Ms?"

I replied, "All." We sat in silence for a little bit. His facial expression didn't change much. I didn't know what to think of his initial response. He got up. He walked over to my desk, and began to write on a post-it. A thousand thoughts rushed through my mind on what he was about to share. When he finished, he stuck the note in plain sight. It simply stated, "I'm in the same boat as you."

I took in a deep breath, and exhaled at full length slowly. Our faces lit up. Sharing the same secret as one another allowed full honesty into the stories that began to pour out from us. We told funny stories recalling why we thought the other might be gay. We reflected upon similar hardships we faced, and discussed how society did not understand gay people and quickly labeled them. We shared the dreams that our families had for us, including having a wife and kids, but how we knew it wouldn't happen. We made a pact to maintain mutual secrecy.

I shared with Alex that I could perhaps see myself coming out in the next couple of years. Our opinions seemingly intertwined until I brought up that topic. Alex raised his eyebrows and then lowered them while looking down. His body language drooped and he shook his head slowly in disagreement. His excitement of coming out to me became deflated at the thought of his family knowing. Alex elaborated on how long he wished to hide his secret.

"I plan to hide this for my entire life," he said. "If I told my family now, they will feel as if I've been lying to them all along, and people would all be disappointed in me because I'm gay, or because I'm a liar."

I empathized with his concern.

"Alex, if and when I do come out one day, I know that I will be faced with much disapproval. I know that I will cause a serious disruption in my life. But I cannot withhold this important piece of myself forever. I don't think you should either, it's not mentally healthy for either one of us."

Alex didn't agree. He simply couldn't fathom coming out to his family. Knowing that this issue wouldn't be solved in one night, we let it rest. Sharing my genuine thoughts, fears, and insecurities recharged my life's energy. I felt as if I had been breathing with one lung my entire life, and suddenly my other lung opened up and allowed me to inhale at full capacity for the very first time. An immeasurable weight lifted off of my shoulders that evening, and we stayed up until past five o'clock in the morning.

The windowsills began to brighten as the sun rose. Our eyes were heavy and our voices were faint after one of the longest conversations of my life. Reality set back in. Alex had to be at class in two hours, and I needed to make my tennis practice. We hugged, and assured one another that things would somehow be ok. A few days later, I received an email from him. It read as follows:

"Adam, a lot of thoughts went through my mind that night when we had our discussion, and the past few days as well. I listened to that Christian song we heard over and over again and found myself in deep thought. I began to really listen to the words, and a flush of vivid images of my life suddenly appeared. In a certain aspect, I was thinking of the days of my innocence, days in which I knew nothing about what pain really was. As I may tell you over and over again, this year has definitely taken a turn on me. As this acceptance of myself may be painful, realizing what I really am is something that I needed. Although this will be a lengthy process for both you and me, we will ultimately make it, because I feel it in my heart. I believe that God allowed us to take part in each other's lives for some reason, and for some reason we were chosen to cross each other's roads. Our voyage will be a tough one, but we will make it all the way through, as a new chapter in our lives begins."

Crush; Crushed

Revealing my secret to Alex allowed me to venture into new conversation topics. I talked about who I liked. I expressed my lifelong suppressed feelings of attraction. I desired to find someone in my daily life that shared similar interests as me. However, I felt that unless I proclaimed "I'm gay!" and so did every other gay guy, it seemed like mission impossible to find someone gay that I liked at college. I never went to any gay bar or club except that one time in Boston, and didn't care to get into that scene yet. Many of my friends dated people at school, and I longed to experience the same thing. I had no idea how it could or would ever work out for me as a closeted gay male, without basically asking someone, "Are you gay? And if so, do you want to have a pact that if we get into a relationship we won't tell anyone?"

News reached me that Toby, one of my friends from my home church, recently came out while at college. Others didn't take it the way he had hoped, and it completely ruined his college experience. Verbal and emotional abuse surrounded him. The backlash proved too difficult on him, and Toby dropped out of school. His college days ended because of his honesty. The reality hit me hard. If I followed this same path, I needed to fully prepare myself for any potential repercussions. I talked through this event with Alex. Even with similar fears, I increasingly felt the need to be true to myself. The risk of damaging myself no longer fully stopped my thought process. My silenced and overlooked heart demanded my attention.

I began to develop feelings for a guy named Brad. I couldn't tell if he was gay, and if so, I certainly didn't know if he had any interest in me either. The guessing game tore me apart. My frustrations grew with each passing day. Part of me still wished that I could just forgo it all and live out a normal and straight life like so many others around me. I knew that being straight wasn't physically or emotionally possible for me, yet part of me still wished so badly that I was. It placed hurt upon my psyche to continually think along that regard.

When I got overwhelmed mentally, I often snuck into the school's chapel late at night to sing and play the piano. One of my female friends, Natalie, came with me. After this late night music session, she went home. I stared around at the beautiful windows in the church, and enjoyed its absolute silence. I placed my right hand upon my head, and rested my elbow on the piano. I closed my eyes. Apprehensions regarding my life's path flooded my mind and quickly overtook the once peaceful silence.

I got up and walked directly across campus towards the tennis courts. The sound of late night crickets filled the humid air. Before reaching the campus's end, I stopped under a telephone pole with a dimly flickering security light. I rested my back against the telephone pole and opened up a notebook from my bag.

"Dear God, thank You first and foremost for everything up to this point in my life. The school I'm at is great as are my friends here, and my loving family is back home. To any outsider I probably look like I have everything going for me, but I couldn't feel any different. Yes, I do have a lot of gifts and blessings, more, surely than I deserve – but I feel empty inside. I strive for love or for any relationship at all. Tonight, while playing the piano with Natalie, I wanted so badly to just feel something, anything at all. I wanted to be singing and playing for someone who I could be attracted to. I wanted to flirt with someone that I actually had feelings for. I wanted to learn what it was like to be in a relationship, to feel love or anything like it. There I was with a gorgeous, tall, athletic girl beside me, as nice as they come, and I felt absolutely nothing. Nothing at all Lord. It still breaks my heart. It absolutely crushes me like a stone and breaks me down as a person. I wish that I could bring a girl like this home to my parents, and introduce her as my girlfriend, but it will never happen. Perhaps I have finally realized that, but I need Your help to do so too God. Please help me realize and appreciate everything around me, and not take what I have for granted. But God, please help me find a person for me Lord. I need You and Your love to guide me through my days. I only hope that one day I will find someone on this earth who loves me even a fraction of the amount that You love me. Thank you Lord for the beautiful night and the weather today. Amen."

I tucked my notebook back into my bag. I reflected upon how I recently tackled my biggest fear by finally telling someone about me. I dug up feelings of determination to continue the surge of moving forward in my life. Complacency and stagnancy revealed themselves as my enemies. I needed to find the inspiration and the will to get myself out of this funk and to keep pressing onwards. Over the next few weeks I worked my hardest to do just that, and subsequently I found my feelings of attraction growing for Brad.

We shared limited interactions passing by one another on campus and in the cafeteria. We briefly chatted on a few occasions. Brad had certain tendencies and looks when our eyes connected. He glanced at me out of the corner of his eyes even after I passed by. The feeling of attraction seemed mutual, but I hesitated to give too much away. It felt like a metaphorical game of chess. We stalemated, and nobody wanted to make a move. I spent an excessive amount of time analyzing the situation. I felt trapped in a world where I couldn't express myself. Alex expressed that he too thought Brad was gay.

My heart absolutely ached and my stomach constantly turned through this back and forth race of how I felt and what I thought of Brad's orientation. I longed to finally experience affection, after a life filled with emptiness and lies up to that point. For months, I quite literally drove myself crazy. My nights became restless. I couldn't focus upon my class work, and blankly stared through my Professors as they spoke. Dealing with my hidden sexuality remained hard enough, but the entire situation with Brad doubled my dose of anxiety. Speaking with Alex only got me so far.

I couldn't take it any longer. I had to make a decision. Either I walk away from the situation and cut off all interactions with Brad, or I just go for it. As the unforgiving clock of life kept ticking, I faced the fact that I would need to accept the consequences from the situation at hand, good or bad. One evening, Brad and I chatted online. I told him,

"Brad, I'm glad I got to meet you. You're a pretty cool guy."

"Thanks, you as well," he shared.

I stalled. I asked how his classes went and made small talk. My feet shook excessively on the floor and my fingers hovered over the keyboard not knowing which keys to land upon. I clenched my hands tight, and then stretched my fingers out wide. I worked up the courage to type the following message,

"I'd like to get to know you better…"

It took all of my strength to hit the "send" button, but I did. He asked what I meant. At a complete loss for words, I froze. The time on his last message said 9:37pm, and I watched the clock on my computer until it hit 9:42pm. In those five minutes, I hadn't come up with anything intelligent or witty to say. I scratched my head and tapped my fingertips along my forehead repetitively.

"I have feelings for you," I said.

I heard every one of my heart's beats. It felt like a roaring machine trying to burst out of my chest. My eyes locked onto the computer screen in disbelief of what I just sent. For the very first time in my life, I genuinely told someone that I liked them. I read and re-read my message. I stalked the status on the conversation window that showed, "Brad is typing a response..." then, nothing. Again, this happened a few more times, implying he typed up a response and then deleted it before sending.

I didn't know how to interpret this. I had no idea what went through his head or how he would respond. My shoulders rose with tension and I unsuccessfully tried to slow down my breathing. My eagerness to receive his response quickly got overshadowed by my fears of receiving a negative reply. Two minutes passed. I became horrified. My esophagus seemed to shrink as my breathing tightened. His response finally came in.

"I'm flattered Adam, but I'm not gay. I'm sorry."

I covered my face in disbelief. My hands then fell down to my desk and made a loud thud. All of my strength left my body and I depended upon the chair and the desk to keep me upright. Every single fear I envisioned for months came true with one brief response from Brad. Every single hope for my potential with him fled. I couldn't formulate a response. I didn't know what to do. Panicking, I apologized, and shut my computer. I turned the lights off in my room and laid in my bed, staring up towards the ceiling with my eyes wide open in disbelief. Heavy thoughts felt like chains holding me down to the bed. They immobilized me.

How could I have so badly misread this whole situation? How could something that felt so right turn out to be so cold and end so abruptly? What if he told his friends about me, or worse yet, my friends? What if this ruined my college days like my friend Toby's? I obsessed over the repercussions. I instantly regretted my boldness and stupidity. My head spun around in circles and couldn't grasp what had just unfolded. In conjunction with my fears of others finding out, my heart ached for a relationship that it hoped for with Brad over the past few months. I was completely crushed. I immediately picked up the phone and called Alex.

"Adam, I still think he is gay," he said. "He's probably just scared and afraid to reveal himself if he's not fully ready. I'm not ready to let go of my identity yet either."

Perhaps Alex was right. That didn't stop the hurt though. I had an immensely difficult time fully accepting this result, after having invested so many emotions and thoughts in it for months. With an aching heart and a feeling of desolateness, I found myself in a really low place. I worried about the future of my life, my extended family of Christians completely against homosexuality, my friends' perceptions of me, and the fact that I still hadn't experienced a relationship all at once. On top of it, I felt absolutely embarrassed beyond belief. I walked around campus with my head low, fearing to see Brad. I changed my routes to the cafeteria on days that I knew we crossed paths.

A week or so later, one of my biggest fears came true. Brad told a few of his friends at school what happened. One of his friends, Lauren, also attended the same high school that I did. Like a storm taking shape with visible warning, I wanted nothing else but to avoid it, but I couldn't. I felt completely helpless and vulnerable. Being outed on someone else's terms placed feelings of depression, misery, and horror into my being. I interacted with Lauren occasionally, but she and I weren't too close in high school due to being a grade level apart. But what if she told some of our mutual high school friends? Which of these friends knew my good friends? And with my family being so close to so many people in my hometown, what if they found out?

My mindset and outlook on my future changed. My confidence level dropped to an all time low. My self-worth disappeared. I walked around campus in sweatpants, a hooded sweatshirt with the hood up, and a baseball hat on. I didn't want to exist. My once positive demeanor and extroverted personality became replaced with nervousness and reserve. I didn't want to hang out with my friends, and I isolated myself for weeks. My inability to sleep affected my tennis game. Each time my phone rang from my parents, my heart trembled with fear. What did they know? Why were they calling? I didn't know how to go on.

Stepping Back – Easter 2006

I deeply cherished holidays with my family. They centered me and filled me with love. Whether still young and living at home or visiting from college, holidays always proved some of the most special times of the year. Easter 2006 came at a great time for me. I removed myself from school for a few days. However, I had recently contracted bronchitis. During this same time frame, it compounded by on setting laryngitis, and a pretty major sinus infection as well. I lost my voice. I couldn't participate with my cousins and family in our normal non-stop joking manner. I became a spectator to the day's festivities, a new role for me in my family setting.

Easter dinner, like all holiday meals cooked by my Mom, was simply fantastic. I filled my stomach to the brim. Without partaking in conversation, I felt like a complete outside observer to the spectacle of conversation and food flying across the table in front of me. My family gestured like air traffic controllers landing airplanes. The decibel level amplified with constant laughter. I smiled, and thanked God for each member of my loving family.

Earlier in the day, we attended an Easter service as a family. The Pastor delivered a powerful sermon about Jesus' resurrection for each and every one of us. "Jesus didn't judge," he said. "He didn't turn people down. No matter your age, race, gender, or economic status, Jesus died for you. He rose from the grave for you; thus the celebration of Easter."

The Pastor discussed how humans tend to categorize or judge people, and how Jesus never did any of that. "We should live like Him!" the Pastor so boldly proclaimed. While seated at the dinner table and reflecting upon this message, I recalled another sermon from the same Pastor just a few months prior. In that sermon, he preached against homosexuality. The irony struck me, and I realized that the belief of not discriminating against anyone perhaps didn't apply to me. Though the Easter sermon originally inspired me, it then confused me. Did Jesus die for all of us, or just *most* of us? I became accustomed to look for this tiny hidden asterisk that placed gay people outside of church's "all inclusive" mantras.

Wrestling between the thoughts of love, faith, and acceptance, the message and the holiday meal posed a standing contradiction for me. Did my church and family fully love and accept me, or did they not? I helped clean the dishes, and headed up to my room. I picked up my notebook that I used as a journal. I outlined the pros and cons of coming out, and the potential troubles it may cause within my family and life. I weighed the importance of my happiness vs. the importance of other people's perceptions of me. I flipped to a blank page. I formed three columns, and placed a title above each of them: God, family, and self. I wrote the word "betrayal" under each of these in bold font.

I felt completely stuck, in a lose-lose-lose situation. Changing my sexual orientation appeared the only plausible solution to provide guaranteed happiness. I refused. After years of failed attempts and misery, I needed to slam that door shut. I got up and walked over to the mirror in my bedroom. With bloodshot eyes, tears began rolling down my face. I grabbed the counter below the mirror firmly, and stared at myself deeply. I hated the look of myself crying.

"Feeling bad for yourself never got you anywhere!" I said through clenched teeth.

I shook my head and asked God for help. I wiped away my tears. I walked over to my bed, sat down, and reopened my journal. I flicked the top off the pen. I made a big "X" through the three columns, and covered each of my entries of the word 'betrayal' by aggressively scratching the pen back and forth. I ripped the page out, and crumbled it up. I enacted a staring contest with a blank page in front of me. After a few minutes of thought, I wrote in the biggest font that I could fit on the page "OVERCOME IT." I slammed the notebook shut, and tossed it across my bedroom floor.

First Relationship

During the second half of my junior year at school, I felt sparks between one particular guy and myself. This time around, I approached the situation with extreme caution. However, it became increasingly obvious to me that the interest and attraction between Kevin and I grew silently and mutually. The guessing game and uncertainties continued with each of our muted interactions. We flirted with one another just enough to stay under the radar of suspicion. Handshakes hello and hugs goodbye lasted a split second longer than normal. I fell for him.

One night, Kevin and I hung out with our friends. Momentarily, just the two of us remained in the room. I played it cool. We sat next to one another, and the feelings between us seemed blatant. I moved my chair closer to his, and we made small talk. As if something took over my body, I suddenly reached out and brushed his knee slightly with my right hand. Without hesitation, he pulled my hand towards him and we embraced. We hugged so tightly that my lungs constricted, but I didn't care. Excitement, joy, and relief took over my body. Smiling, I pointed my right pointer finger towards him and said,

"I knew that you were gay!"

"I wasn't so sure about you," Kevin said, "but hoped that you were too!"

A glimpse of hope revealed itself in my life. I tossed the weight of the world from my shoulders, and felt for the first time that I might actually have a chance at finding happiness. Soon after, a few friends walked back into the room. I tried to maintain my composure, and disguised my absolute elation. I went to bed that evening with the happiest mindset I had in years. I couldn't stop smiling. Subsequently, in the next couple of weeks, we secretly dated. I entered into my first relationship.

My secrets doubled. In addition to disguising my sexuality from the world, I now disguised my first ever boyfriend, too. Ironically, I felt somewhat self-assured in who I had become, but never before had I acted so diligently to hide myself from others. I did so to the stage of complete paranoia. Though overjoyed at finally experiencing affection with someone, we completely masked our feelings for one another in public. We turned our emotions and feelings on and off constantly, as if a valve controlled them.

Our friend groups intertwined. Our paths crossed more and more. After an out of state tennis tournament, I returned back to Siena. Kevin and I met up for brunch in our school cafeteria with some friends. I wanted nothing more than to reach out and hug or kiss him, but I resisted the urge. We gave one another a handshake hello. We quietly brushed each other's feet under the table. I wanted to jump out of my seat and properly greet my boyfriend hello, but I didn't.

We finished eating, and the group disbanded. Kevin and I found privacy in a distant part of campus. Without anyone around, we functioned like a normal couple. We held hands. We spoke affectionate words to one another. I truly felt bipolar, switching back and forth between different versions of myself. As difficult as it was to contain my emotions while in public, my internal happiness shined like never before. Temporarily letting go of my lifelong suppressed feelings, attractions, and emotions evoked absolute euphoria. I felt like a caged bird let out of confinement for the very first time.

The dance of hiding ourselves continued for a couple of months. We expressed "I love you" to one another. In the midst of my first true relationship, I placed a lot of emotional dependency upon Kevin. The semester neared completion, and summer approached. We shared our fears and concerns regarding our families finding out about us. We talked about how to combat the distance and separation. We eagerly anticipated returning to one another after the break concluded.

Summer began. We exchanged emails, texts, and phone calls daily. Everything went smoothly. I worked at the family business during the days, and maintained my life of secrecy in the confines of my room at night. As the weeks progressed, our conversations became further apart. We shared less affection verbally and in writing with one another. About one month into our almost four month long summer break, I didn't hear back from Kevin for an entire day. I anxiously yet patiently awaited for a response from him the following day. Again, nothing. My concern and confusion grew. Another day passed, and another one yet. Day after day, week after week, I heard nothing from him. Thoughts rampaged through my mind. Did I offend him in some way? Did we break up? Did something happen to him physically and he's hurt or worse? The questions and uncertainties ate away at my mind like an illness. My emotions exponentially weakened with the passing of each day.

I became absolutely restless and constantly on edge. My heart learned a new level of hurt. It tested my limits to try and deal with this constant pain privately. I wanted to drive the few hour drive to his house and ask him what happened, but I knew that it wouldn't solve anything. Pushing myself into the picture more than my texts, calls, and emails had already done wouldn't help. My mind grew weary. My feet felt like cement blocks that dragged underneath me. Each time I escaped my family and found a private room, my head collapsed into my hands. My eyes swelled and I hunched over. I grabbed at my gut to remove the imaginary knife that tore me apart from the inside. After finally landing a loving relationship that I longed for my entire life, I was instantly left alone. The pain and internal anguish surpassed the pain of my hidden sexuality alone. Something had to give. I could no longer deal with it all on my own.

A Crack in the Planet

With a completely broken heart, no communication from the guy that told me he loved me, and the discomfort of still living under my parent's roof without them knowing they had a gay son, it all proved too much to handle. I put on a smile around my family and while working at the business, but I felt far from myself. I couldn't suppress my pain and depression much longer.

Being a family owned and operated business, I took things to heart when customers abused or damaged our property. After all, fixing damages, especially the very costly go-karts, was both pricey and timely for our extremely hard working family. One day, a teenager aggressively bumped his friends while on our go-karts. He rammed into our metal guardrails surrounding the track. The sounds of the metal go-kart smashing into the rails and his friend's karts set me off. I repeatedly warned him to cut it out.

"What do you think you're doing? I told you five times to not bash the car like that."

"Whatever man, calm down," he said. "I paid the stupid six dollars, I can do what I want."

"What you can do is get off the track and out of the facility. If you want to cause damage like that to our property, it's not going to be on my watch."

He unbuckled his seatbelt and stood up out of his go-kart. Three of his friends stopped their karts behind him and did the same.

"This asshole is trying to rip me off!" he yelled back at his friends while waving his hands in the air. "He's trying to cut our time short."

I took a few deliberate steps directly towards him. He stood a couple inches taller than me, but I stood chest to chest with him. I looked up at him and clenched my jaw. I squeezed my fists. I tilted my neck forward and shouted, "Get the hell off the property before I drag you out myself."

He turned back at his friends to see their reaction. I leaned in closer to him and breathed in deeply and exhaled loudly. Adrenaline pumped through my veins and my whole upper body slightly shook. He aggressively raised both of his middle fingers in my face and yelled, "Fuck you!" as he walked off the track.

I wanted nothing more than to fight him and his entire group of friends all at once. Damaging my family's property, on top of everything else going on in my life, sent me over the edge. I checked my emotions, and walked away from the situation. They left the premise, squealing their tires in the parking lot.

I paced back and forth with anger. I walked back to our house instead of the snack bar. One of the employees at the business caught wind of what happened, and notified my parents. Shortly thereafter, they arrived at home. They walked in to find me completely distraught in tears, still shaking from the situation that just unfolded. They tried to speak with me, but I didn't return their attempts at conversing. I couldn't look them in the eyes. They asked what happened and why I sat in front of them sobbing. I signaled for them to please leave me alone. I rushed away and went down to our basement.

They tried to get me to let go of the situation, and encouraged me not to let some stupid teenagers affect me so much. I struggled to speak and made no coherent sentences in between my distressed replies. I desperately wanted them away from me at that moment, yet I needed them for so many reasons that they did not yet know. I headed towards the back room in our basement. My parents followed with their looks of concern growing by the minute. I grabbed my head with both hands and yelled, "Just leave me alone!"

They didn't. I resorted to the last possible room I could find. Tucked away in the back corner of the basement and left unfinished, it housed the HVAC system and a large humidifier. Cold, damp concrete walls surrounded me. Only a tiny bit of light managed to enter into the room through a small window in the room's corner. For the first time in my life, with quite literally my back up against the wall, I thought about telling my parents about me once and for all.

My Mom began to ask me some questions. She tried to put me at ease and guess the problem on my overly troubled mind.

"Are you in some sort of trouble?"

Still unable to speak, I shook my head 'no' as the tears flew down my face. My body began to quiver.

"Do you have concerns for your health?"

"No," I replied.

Thoughts raced through my mind of what I would do if they asked me if I was gay. My current state of extreme vulnerability blocked my rationality.

"Did you get a girl pregnant?" they asked.

"No."

"Did you hurt someone or something or do something bad honey?" my Mom asked. She worriedly leaned in towards me for my reply.

Five minutes of this agony passed. They again asked if it had something to do with a girl or a girlfriend. My mind felt absolutely defeated. I couldn't work up the courage to speak the words myself, and I felt as if they would never understand it even if I could. Feelings of courage remotely surfaced in the back of my mind, trying to combat my fears. My mind entered war with itself. My emotions swirled and my knees weakened. I glanced up at my parents, the two most loving parents that anyone could ever ask for. My mind wouldn't allow my lips to speak, no matter which words I tried to use. I closed my eyes and drooped my head, silently shaking it back and forth. Faintly, I heard the words,

"Are you gay?"

My body partially collapsed to the floor and I held myself up with my hands. I nodded my head 'yes' before my brain could even comprehend or process how to reply.

"That's alright, you can change..." I heard my Father say.

Through my sobbing tears, I spoke clearly for the first time.

"No I can't!" I angrily replied.

My Mom elbowed my Dad slightly in the gut. The statement temporarily confirmed my entire lifelong fear of not being understood, or able to justify that I naturally was gay. My eyes swelled up to the point where I could no longer see clearly. I hunched over the floor while trying to catch my breath. Statements began to pour out from my parents.

"It's ok Adam, we still love you honey," they said. "Did you think that we wouldn't if you told us this?"

"I don't know," I whispered, wiping my runny nose.

"How long have you known? Why haven't you talked about this before with us?"

I answered their questions. I even told them I had a boyfriend at school.

"He hasn't talked to me in weeks. I don't know what happened," I said.

They glanced at one another while trying to take in all of my revelations. They expressed repeatedly just how much they loved me and that everything would somehow be ok. I particularly felt concern for my Dad, as I was the only male child in our Italian-American family. I felt like I let them down. They did the best they could to comfort me, and led me up to our living room and turned on the TV.

"Take the rest of the day off honey, and just relax. Everything will be ok, we promise."

Later that evening, Tiffany and I hung out in our separate bedrooms before dinner. I entered the hallway.

"Can I talk to you?"

She put down her book.

"What's going on?" she asked, with a concerned voice.

"Tiff, I'm gay…"

"Ok. Do you know what's for dinner?"

I looked at her with pure shock. I couldn't comprehend her initial statement. She feared something worse.

"I obviously picked up that a major event unfolded in the house today. You cried all day and Mom and Dad kept telling me that everything was fine. I thought you had cancer or a terminal illness or something."

We embraced in one of the longest hugs of my life. I cried into her shoulder. A slight smile surfaced through my tears as we made our way to the dinner table. We didn't talk about the day's events. My family didn't pretend that they didn't happen; rather they focused upon what did happen. We still had each other. My Dad broke the silence.

"Son, I'd really like you to help me work upon the batting cages tomorrow morning. We can work upon the overhead conveyer belt together, that thing really needs some good work."

"Ok, Dad."

The next morning, we did just that. For two hours before the business opened, he and I did what we came to know and love as a Father and son, an outdoor project. Later, my Mom brought me out to lunch. We tackled some difficult questions. At my request, we agreed to keep my secret from the rest of our family for now. For the first time in my life, I asked my Mom for relationship advice. As a true "Momma's boy" I spilled out my aching heart to her. No answer or advice solved my pain, but discussing it helped to temporarily heal the hurt.

A couple of weeks later, I saw pictures of Kevin online. Alive and well, he appeared happy while with his friends. My mind couldn't comprehend the situation. It deeply troubled me why Kevin unexplainably cut me out of his life. My pain and confusion didn't subside, yet I tried my best to still find enjoyment in the summer. I went to visit a few of my best friends in New York City. We painted the town for three restless days. For the remainder of the summer, I focused upon what I could control, and enjoyed each and every day with my loving family.

I returned to school. Kevin and I had a heart to heart chat. He also came out to his family that summer, with a very different result from mine. Kevin's parents convinced him of a hell-bound fate if he continued down the path that he travelled. They brainwashed him. His eyes, once filled with warmth and love for me, were now filled with cold and confusion. He couldn't look at me while speaking. He believed what his parents told him.

"I'm not gay, Adam," he said. "It's something that I can consciously change. It's just a phase."

Kevin conveyed the message verbally, but his expressions told a different story. His glazed-over eyes blankly stared at the pavement. He forced a smile and a head nod to justify an artificial belief in his very own words. I didn't know that Kevin. His presence mimicked a ghost, a mere representation of what he used to be. I expressed my deepest empathy and concern for what he went through. I also expressed my pain, anger, and confusion from the summer. He apologized. He kept a distance between us, and limited direct eye contact.

During my senior year, we dated again. We never regained what we had. We no longer expressed I love you to one another. The feelings and emotions, which we once expressed so freely, were now tainted with hesitating hearts and words. Kevin experienced heavy cognitive dissonance wrestling between what his parents convinced him of, and his true feelings for me. I approached the situation with my guard up. I ensured that my heart's vulnerability never fell so low with him again. School finished up. I grabbed my Bachelor's degree in business. We took to our separate lives. We grew apart, and lost whatever it was that we tried to regain.

Setting My Sights upon Italy

After college, I aligned my immediate future with what my heart desired most. I strived to fill a gap inside of me. I directly took after my Dad in regards to him setting his eyes upon something and becoming absolutely laser focused to accomplish it. At times, my Mom laughed and rolled her eyes at us. I didn't explore various careers paths or start the job hunt like most recent college graduates. I wanted to live in Italy.

I agreed to work at the family business over the summer in order to save up some money. I spent the summer dedicated to studying Italian and going to language classes with my Grandpa Tony. I got to connect with my Grandpa on a different level. We talked about our family's heritage in Italy and our older relatives both in the U.S. and abroad. My Grandpa's good friend in Schenectady informed me that his granddaughter Lydia lived in Rome.

Lydia and I exchanged emails over the next month or so. A spot opened up in her five person apartment in Rome starting in September. I asked Lydia if she and her roommates would consider me. Everyone agreed. I booked my trip without hesitation. I arranged to take classes in Rome at an Italian school focusing upon language, art, and culture. September arrived. I packed my bags, and set out on my journey to the Fiumicino airport in Rome.

Upon arrival, I looked as touristy as could be. I hauled two large luggage, one carry-on, and hoisted a backpack around my shoulder. I wore tennis shoes, a plain t-shirt and shorts. However, when I stepped foot outside of the airport in Rome, it felt like home. The air contained a slight humidity. Food trucks sold pizza, calzones, and Italian desserts. The delicious smells that filled the air reminded me of my hometown's strip of Little Italy.

The hustle and bustle around the airport with taxis, buses, and plenty of Vespas didn't intimidate me. I parted the seas of people and transportation requests. Lydia worked the day I landed, so one of my other roommates, Carlo, picked me up from the airport. I arrived at our pre-planned meeting spot. Twenty minutes later, an Italian guy around my age stopped at the same location. I hesitantly asked, "Carlo?" In a thick Italian accent he replied, "Adam?"

We smiled and shook hands. He grabbed a few of my bags and loaded them into his car. Carlo had slicked black hair, tight jeans, and sported bright white fashionable shoes. We drove with the windows down. The smell of exhaust filled the air from the mopeds that danced in between the cars, maneuvering their way to the front of each traffic light. American businesses like McDonald's dotted the streets right alongside ancient ruins. Carlo described all of our roommates and the location of our apartment within the city.

Later in the evening, Lydia arrived. We hit it off instantly. Her personality matched that of a comic's, and she rattled off impersonations nonstop. She joked about everything. On the day that I arrived to Italy, world-renowned tenor Luciano Pavarotti passed away from his long battle with pancreatic cancer. The entire country mourned. Lydia introduced me to her Italian friends as, "Adam Mastroianni from New York, the man that killed Pavarotti."

I spent the first evening cooking with Lydia, and enjoyed the Italian conversation at dinner with my new roommates. Lydia spoke the language fluently, and assisted in translations when I got behind. Later, we ventured off to a new nightclub on its first night open in Rome. We stayed out until 4:00am. I rode home on the back of Carlo's moped, and saw the beautifully lit Coliseum at night. I felt like I was on the set of a movie.

On my second day in Rome, Lydia navigated the public transportation system with me and taught me how to reach my school. Afterwards, we walked what seemed like the entire city. We visited the Spanish Steps, the Pantheon, the Coliseum, the Vatican, and many more sites. Lydia's incredible knowledge of Italian history and politics brought the monuments to life. I felt like a kid in a candy shop and just couldn't get enough.

In my new school, I met people from all over the world such as Switzerland, Sweden, Holland, and Australia. I furthered my knowledge of the Italian language and culture over the following week or so, but the pace seemed a bit slow for me. I learned more by completely immersing myself in the culture. I dropped school so that I could put myself in the heart of Italy – with her people.

I practiced the language by chatting with my bus driver each morning on my ride to the city. I frequented the same pizza shop each afternoon. The toppings varied daily from eggplant and ricotta cheese, to buffalo mozzarella and freshly shaved prosciutto. I walked the streets and engaged with street vendors and anyone willing to converse with me. I tested just about every gelato shop along the narrow cobblestone streets of Rome. I felt like a sponge. My Italian improved quicker and more comfortably than ever before.

From my Grandpa Tony's side of the family (the Mastroianni side), I connected with a few relatives before my trip. I travelled outside of Rome to the small village of Pomezia, where the family now lived. My distant cousins Pascolino and Mario picked me up from the train station. At the house, an entire entourage of family members greeted me with nonstop kisses and hugs. We embraced like a grand family reunion, though we hadn't met in person before. My cousin Cinzia then ripped out a piece of scrap paper and placed it upon the dining room table. We drew out a family tree, and traced how our families grew apart over the years in separate countries.

La Nonna (the Grandmother) stood about five feet tall. She had thick glasses with a frame that appeared to have survived quite a few years. She wore black leather gloves with the fingers cut off. She ran the show. Nonna walked over to me and asked all about Grandpa Tony. Pinching my cheeks, she pulled me down towards her face and planted a big kiss in the middle of my forehead. She wrapped her arm around my side and squeezed me tightly. She didn't let me go for five minutes.

We ate antipasti with various meats and cheeses, a salad, and then freshly baked bread. Spaghetti and a delicious thick red sauce soon followed. I completely filled up on a couple servings of the pasta, and cleaned the red spots of sauce from my cheeks and shirt. I used my last piece of bread to wipe my plate clean and soak up any remaining sauce. I leaned back in my chair and patted my full stomach with content.

Ten minutes later, Pascolino came out from the kitchen. He passed around a plate full of large steaks. "There's more…?" I thought. I tried to quietly pass the plate along, but Nonna waved her hands in the air and said in Italian, "We are worried that you are not eating!" I took one, and forced down as much as I could. We had coffee and a tasty after meal liquor, and the meal finally concluded. I recalled a motto that my Mom used to tell me: "The quickest way to a man's heart is through his stomach." The motto certainly proved its truth. My heart fell in love with Italy more each day after every mouthwatering bite of flavor. I returned to my apartment with fresh Polaroid pictures of my distant family in my pockets.

The following day in Rome I stopped at a pay phone and called home with my calling card. I chatted with my Mom and told her stories of the Italian people, food, and various cities that I visited. "Oh honey I wish so badly that I could come and join you," she said.

Then, it hit me. Why couldn't she come and join? The business had already closed for the year. If I could have chosen one person in the entire world to spend time with in Italy, it would have been my Mom. We share such similar interests and passions in people and in food. I begged her.

"I would have to fly to Europe alone," she said. "And plus, it's probably really expensive to book last-minute."

I tried my best to convince her and shot her over an itinerary later that evening. On a whim, Momma Mastroianni booked her flight to Italy. I waited with open arms to greet her at the airport. She appeared tired after the long trip, but her face lit up upon taking her first steps in Rome. Her smiling eyes bounced back and forth from the buildings to the cars to the people. We put her bags up in my apartment, took a brief rest, and planned out the next week of our journey.

My Mom is just like me in regards to wanting to scrap anything too touristy, and rather spend as much authentic time with the people and food that we could. We set out to visit my Uncle Phil's side of the family, and planned our first stay at their Bed and Breakfast in Positano. A large blue bus navigated the countless switchbacks that climbed up the steep hills. Each hairpin turn revealed a glimpse of the shimmering sea below the picturesque Amalfi Coast. Houses jutted out from the rocky hills and the sunlight illuminated their vibrant colors. A man around 60 years old with salt and pepper hair, Filipo, stood at the business's door. He waved both arms in the air welcoming us. He kissed my Mom on the cheeks and proclaimed, "Welcome to Positano!"

My Mom and I shrieked with excitement. We met the rest of the family. Rachele and Jesomina handed us bottled waters. Smiles never left their faces. "Familia!" they said. The entire front of the restaurant opened up to the outside, overlooking the gorgeous and tranquil coast below. Vines grew alongside the restaurant's outdoor railings, and sprouted bright pink flowers. They showed us pictures of their family and asked us all about America. Their smiles and laughter filled the air with immeasurable love.

We unpacked our things, and met in the restaurant for dinner. Rachele's thick and strong fingers worked a ball of fresh dough to prepare the pasta. Jesomina threw fresh clams and mussels into a pan. She passionately tossed in the remaining ingredients and spices. Filipo prepared a fresh fish caught that morning from the sea. "Sit, sit!" they encouraged us.

After observing the spectacle of true Italian's in their element, we sat at our table. The sun slowly set behind the sea, lighting up the sky with a fiery red color. Filipo served us the seafood pasta, and rolled out a squeaky metal cart next to our table. He poured two glasses of red wine. A covered metal serving platter remained on the cart. He revealed its contents, the perfectly cooked fish. He delicately filleted the fish, and gently picked out each small bone with a fork and knife. His hands moved precisely and efficiently like those of a surgeon. We enjoyed one of the most delicious meals we had ever eaten.

The following day, we explored the small villages of Positano and Amalfi. We visited the Amalfi Cathedral, a gorgeous cathedral built over 1,000 years ago. We walked up a long staircase that led to its grand entrance with beautiful bronze doors. Italian marble and stone abundantly decorated the cathedral's intricate design. Outside, vendors sold Italian staple foods like gelato and pizza. Stores sold the region's infamous Limoncello liqueur in a variety of uniquely shaped and colored glass bottles.

After one more evening with the family, we reluctantly said our farewells. The family members and my Mom cried as they shared their loving hugs goodbye. We toured Rome, and spent a few days with Carlo's family in Sicily too. After some of the most memorable days of my life, my Mom's trip soon came to an end.

The friendship between Carlo and I grew over the months we lived together. Gay people often know (or highly suspect) of other gay people. Some call it "gaydar." Carlo appeared completely closeted. I sensed his inner unhappiness and desire to finally tell someone his secret. One evening, I shared my story with him. I wanted to make him feel comfortable. He painfully and hesitantly began to share his story with me. He broke down and cried. Carlo expressed deep concerns regarding his family, his workplace, and his friend circles. We empathized. I received his deepest trust while discussing one of the most difficult admissions of his life.

At the time of my trip in 2007, a select few European countries progressed in regards to LGBT rights. The Netherlands became the first country in the world to allow same sex marriage in 2001. The United States and Italy, like most other countries, did not allow same sex marriage or equal rights for their LGBT citizens. The majority of LGBT people that I met served their lives like I did mine. We maintained an outward image and person to society, and an inner secretive person that only submerged in the safe haven of an LGBT nightclub or while around a trusted group of friends.

Carlo told me stories of how kids taunted and made fun of gay and lesbian people in Italian schools. We discussed the unique hardships he faced while living in the Catholic capital of the world. Our friendship humbled me. Carlo experienced many of the same issues and fears as me, in an entirely different walk of life. My struggles no longer seemed all that unique or isolated. We tried to fathom the oppressing societies that we lived in that would discriminate against us if we came out.

My lifelong fears temporarily lessened through my friendship with Carlo. While stepping outside of my daily routines in America, the world shrunk, and my importance and realization to seek out my own happiness grew. I didn't wish to reveal myself to the entire world just yet, but I felt more so than ever before the desire to genuinely and entirely be myself. My time abroad pushed me to actively grasp some much needed inner peace and understanding.

Living in Italy unlocked part of me as a person. It provided a missing link to my ancestry, and provided one of the most self-discovering and rejuvenating times of my life. I truly fell in love with the city of Rome and its people and culture. Nearing the end of my trip, I actively thought about calling it my new full-time home. However, just as I began to pursue gaining dual citizenship through my Grandfather's bloodline, some bad news arrived. Grandpa Tony wasn't doing so well back home. His cancer returned with a vengeance. I temporarily forewent the process of gaining my Italian citizenship, and returned home immediately.

Ti Amo, Ti Amo Sempre

My Grandpa Tony fought kidney cancer hard. He went through multiple surgeries and recurrences, and less than one of his kidneys remained. His health fluctuated after a few years of this battle. The cancer spread aggressively. It no longer localized, and developed into leukemia. The doctors explained that there would not be an operation or a next procedure, but rather the beginning of the inevitable end. He pushed through everything with a positive spirit and attitude. Grandpa spent many evenings with us having family dinners and helping with chores around the business, as he had done for as long as I could remember.

A few weeks prior to Christmas 2007, I stopped by his shoe-shop in Schenectady where he worked and seemed his normal self. He mentioned that he had to go various doctors for his next set of appointments. My Grandpa's strength and resiliency made me think not much of it. I denied the facts. I optimistically and persistently thought that there must be a fix or a cure or a way that he would somehow get through it. I simply couldn't imagine life without him in it.

Although his doctors tried what they could, my Grandpa's health faded quickly. One month after visiting him at work, he fell to the opposite end of the spectrum of life. I unwillingly learned what hospice care meant. I visited him in his living room in a recliner chair. His strength rapidly departed from his body. I slowly fed him soup. I combed his hair and trimmed his thin grey mustache as we chatted. He looked handsome like he always had. He silently endured through the pain.

Two days later, both his breathing pattern and heart rate began to weaken. His body functions gave up on him. My heart ached to see him struggling to breathe. He faded quickly. We voiced to him, "It's OK to let go" and not to hold on for us. Through our tears, we told him how much we loved him. His breathing became even slower. He voiced his last words, "Ti amo, Ti amo sempre," or, "I love you, I love you always." My family held him in our hands. We told him that we couldn't wait to see him again in heaven.

Surrounded by the strongest people in my life, it deeply troubled me to see them all weeping so uncontrollably. We comforted one another, and said our goodbyes to Grandpa. I pressed my fingers gently into his wrist as to feel his pulse. Thud-thud. His heart rate was slow, slow and weak. Thud…thud. Time extended in-between the beats, and the strength continued to noticeably decrease. Thud ..... *thud*. I felt my Grandpa's very last heartbeat.

Everyone hysterically cried. I heard my family's pain-filled voices and saw their sobbing tears. I experienced an unexpected emotion. As tears silently rushed down my face, I felt such clarity in the midst of such hysteria. I ran my hand along his hair, knowing that he finally rested in peace. I felt so incredibly honored to have had him as my Grandfather, and so honored to be right there next to him in the time of his passing. I thanked the Lord that my Grandpa passed so gently and peacefully.

I didn't know how to manage losing the person that I considered my role model, my hero, and my friend. Like a keystone, Grandpa Tony held together our bridge of life, love, and family. The loss devastated my family. For days on end, the tears wouldn't stop. I appreciated spending so many years with such an incredible man that forever shaped my very being. My Grandpa forever influenced my values on family, the importance of love, and the motivation behind working hard for what you want in life.

I set out on a mission to write a book about my Grandpa. I kept it a complete secret to my family except my Mom. The book had to be bigger than just my perspectives and stories. I wanted to gather memories about him from his closest friends throughout his life. The gathering at his wake would be the perfect opportunity to reach this unique crowd and information. Between the restless days of grieving, I found healing and peace planning a project to commemorate his incredible life. I created a letter that asked people to share stories, memories, quotes, pictures, or anything that they remembered about my Grandpa. I filled out a large number of envelopes with my return address on them with this "secret" letter inside.

At the wake, I positioned myself last in the line, with a clear vision of my Mother down the line. As each person approached, my Mom signaled to me when to hand a letter out. The extensive line of people spoke volumes to the influence my Grandpa had on the community, his family, and his friends.

For six months, I anxiously ran to check the mailbox each morning. Every day felt like Christmas. I received photographs, favorite sayings from my Grandpa, and memories and stories that ranged from the 1940s to the early 2000s. Some even left me their telephone numbers. I connected with them to hear their memories of my Grandpa firsthand.

I worked with my Grandpa's lifelong best friend Nat on the ending of the book. Nat detailed his 70+ year friendship with my Grandpa, including memories from the joys of their weddings to the hardships they faced through the days of WWII. I received inspiration for the name of the book from my ex-Professor and now good friend Deb, and found a self-publishing book company online to print out the final work.

I placed my order in early December, and received a large shipment of books a week later. I called my Mom to get her massive Rolodex of addresses. I wrapped each book, and sent them out to arrive in time for Christmas – including instructions not to open until Christmas morning. On Christmas day, family members and friends in various parts of the country opened the book: Letters to Anthony: Memoirs of a Humble Man's Journey through Life, Love, and Family. His inspiration and influence lives on through both the memories he created and those that he has forever impacted.

Returning to Europe

Life blurred following my Grandpa's passing. My family rushed to
get the Sportplex open for another year of business in the spring.
We supported one another and spent much time with my Grandma
Bernie. My Grandma kept herself busy with her various clubs, choir
practices, and hobbies. She lovingly encouraged us all to live out
our lives to the fullest. Once the business opened in April, I did just
that. I set my sights on Spain.

Italian and Spanish share many similar roots and
conjugations. After learning Italian, I could read Spanish pretty
well, without having any previous study of the language. Many
cities and states in the U.S. continued to see an increase in their
Hispanic populations, and an increase in the amount of people that
spoke Spanish accordingly. I wanted to expand my skill-set to
match this trend.

I discovered a company that specialized in placing
Americans throughout the world. In exchange for teaching a person
or persons English, free meals and housing were provided. Two
months later, the company informed me that I matched very well
with a Spaniard family. The family had a mom, dad, and two sons
ages ten and twelve.

I worked diligently over the summer to set myself up for
success. I prepared materials to teach English. I took a Spanish

class at a local Community College. I worked at the family business, and budgeted for my upcoming trip to allow for travel around Europe. Lastly, I pushed myself academically, as per the advice and one of the last wishes of my Grandpa.

"You've got to get that Master's degree, Adam," my Grandpa once said. "You're Bachelor's degree is terrific, it will set you apart from many people out there. But so many people now have their Bachelor's, that the Master's is becoming the new Bachelor's. You need to set yourself even further apart from the crowd."

I didn't want to follow his advice, after spending my entire life in school. I still didn't know what the heck I wanted to do with my life, and continuing on with education seemed silly to me. However, with my Grandpa Tony's voice echoing in the back of my mind, I honored one of his last life's requests that he placed upon me. A business degree would be the strongest choice to add to my resume, and I coupled it with my love for travel. I adamantly researched MBA programs with a minor in International Business.

One big exam stood in my way before gaining entrance to a Master's program in business, the Graduate Management Admission Test (GMAT). Alongside my Spanish language materials and my growing pile of English materials for teaching, I accumulated some hefty books for my GMAT preparation during the summer.

On my last night home in New York, my Mom cooked my favorite meal, spaghetti and meatballs. Her homemade sauce simmered on our stove for the entire day. It's distinct aroma filled the air. Each time I passed through the kitchen, I stirred the sauce and snuck a spoonful of it. The smell and taste distinctly reminded me of my childhood.

Two airplanes and three train-rides later, my host father Carlos picked me up in Spain. Carlos spoke about five words in English, but his welcoming demeanor put me at ease. We instantly got along and found a common interest to discuss, tennis. He drove 140 kilometers/hour on the highway. I didn't know the exact conversion but I sure felt the velocity. I looked out my window and clenched onto the handle above me. The ride lasted 30 minutes, and we arrived outside the city center of Zaragoza, one of Spain's larger cities.

We arrived around dinnertime to the house. Towering white stucco walls held up an impressive red Mediterranean-style roof. The large yard contained olive and fig trees. A friendly white and brown dog greeted me. The view from the house resembled picturesque countryside. I met my host mother Mamen and the two sons. I experienced my first meal cooked by Mamen's mother, a mouthwatering baked chicken and roasted potatoes dish. I quickly acclimated to their unique "*th*" pronunciation in many of their words. For example, in Central and South American Spanish the word "gracias" is stated. In Spain, they say gra*th*ias.

During my first week, I worked with Mamen and established a routine for study times with the kids after school. The boys didn't speak much English, but had very sharp minds. I mixed lessons with activities that they enjoyed, like playing ping-pong or tennis. I worked upon my Spanish during the mornings, studied for the GMAT during the day, and taught the kids English in the evenings.

I desired to boost up my resume for grad school by gaining direct international experience. Mamen previously worked for one of Zaragoza's largest wine producers, and knew the family that owned the winery. I asked if she would arrange a meeting. Mamen obliged, but warned me that the family was a complete mess. She told me they were extremely nice, but very disorganized and rather strange.

I met the family and many workers around the beautiful winery. Endless barrels of wine were housed in extremely large buildings and basements. I discussed my skill-sets in business, and offered my time as a volunteer for a couple of months. They considered the offer, and said they would be in touch. One of the family members then entered the room. Her face expressed pure panic. She rapidly yelled out commands in Spanish. They forget to make a couple hundred bottles of a wine for a wedding the following morning. They put me to work.

Mamen and I scrambled to assist. We grabbed bottles, filled them up, sealed them, placed labels upon them, and wrapped them for the wedding. Everyone freaked out about not finishing on time. I couldn't understand half of their barking orders in Spanish. They induced a high state of stress within the room. While trying to take instructions quickly, I fumbled and dropped a couple bottles of wine on the cold concrete floor. The red wine spread out quickly all across the floor, and shards of glass went everywhere. It looked like a crime scene with a large, growing pool of blood spilled all over. People moved as to not get red wine on their shoes. Someone rushed to get a mop and cleaning supplies. I felt incredibly terrible and embarrassed. My face and the wine distinctly matched in color.

Other workers continued scrambling to make more and more of the bottles. Mamen, seeing how embarrassed I was, began to die laughing. She silently laughed so hard that tears started coming down her face. I did the same. We shouldn't have been laughing, but for some reason it made us laugh even harder and soon became uncontrollable. For five minutes, I couldn't see straight my eyes were filled with so many tears. Mamen ducked around the corner, bent over at the hip, and grabbed at her stomach. It took every ounce of energy in my body to not let out the screams of laughter that built up within me. I looked down and continued to pass wine bottles down the conveyer belt. The family remained more concerned with yelling at one another than to notice we hadn't helped while attempting to regain our composure.

Mamen later told me that it was good luck to break a bottle of wine in that place. Whether it was the broken glass or the free labor I offered, they hired me on. I became their international marketing specialist, and helped to increase their foreign market sales to countries like Great Britain and Qatar. I sipped wine at their wine tasting events, and only pretended to use the spit bucket. As my Spanish improved, I even got to do my best at performing Spanish-English translations for their internationally visiting clientele.

Defining My Purpose

Three years prior to my trip in 2008, gay marriage became legalized in Spain, just the third country in the world to do so. Mamen often ranted on various topics. One day, she voiced to me her disapproval of gay marriage. Her words intensified. I couldn't understand every detail she said, but soon heard the following question,

"Can you believe that two men, or two women can now marry in this country?"

She looked at me, trying to elicit an emotional response. I nonchalantly shrugged my shoulders. I stayed quiet and remained without an opinion on the subject. She continued,

"Gay people are now allowed to adopt children as well," she said. "The nerve. Do you really think that perverts should be the ones bringing up our country's children? This country is headed straight to hell."

She used slurs in the conversation that I understood very well. Words comparable to "faggot" repeatedly came out of her mouth. She judged and discriminated me unknowingly. Her words filled me with anger. Part of me wanted to tell her off, but I resisted. I lived in a foreign country under a stranger's roof, and had no other means for housing or meals. It wasn't my place. My mind flashed back to Lucas whom I met in Boston a few years prior. I empathized with him. I couldn't imagine growing up in a hostile environment like this, with a mother or a family that filled the air with thoughts of hatred towards an entire group of people. I feared his consequence, being kicked out of my house, so I kept my mouth shut.

It greatly disturbed me to hear Mamen utilize this same language in front of her two children. Like sponges, they often repeated their mother's words. One day while watching TV, the boys called a man on TV a fag. They laughed at him together. I shut the TV off and strayed from our lesson. I told them to not use that language in front of me and not to call people hurtful names. They reluctantly agreed as they rolled their eyes. I never did so in front of Mamen however, as to not disrespect her house or her rules.

It disappointed me to see them growing up with this mentality and ingrained prejudice from such a young age. Carlos never stood up to Mamen's rants against gay people. He either agreed and went along, or disagreed and didn't want to stand up to the woman of the house. I couldn't tell. Either way, I kept my secret comfortably stowed away.

I reflected upon the select few that knew about me: Alex, my parents and sister, and a couple of close friends from Siena. My personal comfort level slowly grew, yet abruptly halted in unknown environments. It was eye opening to be around people from different countries and cultures around the world. Why were people so afraid of diversity? What led some people to be understanding and accepting of minorities, and others to be reserved and condemning? I witnessed my personal transformation from my once cocooned-self to someone more accepting of diversity, including my very own. The concept fascinated me.

I contacted my friend Deb, and she and I set out on a new venture in our friendship. We established a goal to publish an academic article together. One would think travelling abroad automatically led someone to be inclined to be more open to diverse cultures, people, and experiences. We wanted to prove this hypothesis, and materialize our thinking through empirical data and research.

Our study of several hundred undergraduate students from around the world confirmed a significant correlation supporting our hypotheses. Individuals who participated in an international educational experience prior to graduating from college were more likely to seek out career opportunities in a diverse work environment. Through more than a year's worth of research and collaborated efforts, we finalized our work: "The Causes and Effects of a Study Abroad Experience: Changing Attitudes towards Cultural Diversity and Careers." We published, and presented our work at the Institute of Behavioral and Applied Management the following year in San Francisco, California.

Travelling abroad expanded my horizons. It unlocked parts of my self-identity, and fueled my desire to further understand world cultures and prejudices. It allowed me to explore academic and personal interests. It exposed me to numerous concepts of both love and hate firsthand. I needed to discover my very own truths in my life and define its purpose. I could no longer stand on the sidelines and take in what others told me as truths without my own exploration. Some people spread rumors. Some people spread hate. I determined to spread truth. I determined to spread love.

Shedding Back Another Layer

Soon after my return to the U.S., I took the GMAT. I hit the threshold I needed in order to be a competitive candidate for business school, and anxiously prepared my applications. I researched programs throughout the country, and had my mind set upon attending the University of Miami, St. John's University in NYC, or the University of Denver. I chose Denver as one of my schools because of their terrific program, beautiful city, and outdoor lifestyle. My sister landed a job with the Denver Broncos two years prior, and I looked forward to potentially moving closer to her as well. We missed each other greatly. I gained acceptance to my top choices, and leaned towards the University of Denver. I excitedly began planning life with Tiffany.

Getting my MBA was going to cost me between $75,000 – $100,000 between pricey tuition and living expenses, even with partial scholarships. One evening, I stumbled across the University of Massachusetts' MBA program. I somehow missed it during my original search. I noticed a unique aspect of their program: they offered their student's full or partial graduate or teaching assistantships in place of scholarships.

A day before the application deadline hit for UMass, I wrote a few more essays and submitted my application online for the measly $40 fee. I didn't expect to hear back. One week later, a call with a Massachusetts area code popped up on my phone. I answered it out of curiosity. An admissions counselor identified herself from UMass' graduate office. We chatted for a few minutes. She asked,

"Ok Adam, do you want me to make your day?"

"Sure?" I replied.

"You've been accepted to the University of Massachusetts MBA program!" she proclaimed.

"That's great!" I said, with halfhearted excitement. My mind had already been made up to attend the University of Denver.

"You have also been chosen as a full recipient of our graduate assistantship program. The University of Massachusetts would like to extend you an offer for two years of tuition, health care benefits, and a stipend to live off of while you attend our program!"

I shook my head in utter disbelief. I tried to make sense of what just happened. After I hung up the phone, I looked like I just saw a ghost. I couldn't comprehend the news all at once. My feelings of elation were quickly masked by feelings of sadness, realizing my dream of moving to Denver most likely wouldn't come true. Reality set in. I couldn't turn the offer down. Though reluctant at first, I aligned my path with UMass' belief in me academically. I trusted God and let go of my innate desires to try and control my future. I eagerly accepted their offer and began the program in the fall.

I continued to visit Tiffany in Denver during my time at UMass. I visited a gay bar during one of my trips. I met a guy, Jake, and we exchanged numbers. Soon after, he and I entered into a long distance relationship. We visited one another a few times over the following year. He wasn't yet out to his family or friends. Between my trips to Colorado and his trips to Massachusetts, we grew weary of constantly hiding our secret. While he visited at UMass, I introduced him as my "friend" to all of my classmates. Although it became natural to do so, it felt like such a disservice to him, and to us. Even after some personal growth following my relationship with Kevin, I remained stuck in time. My paranoia heightened around my new classmates with Jake. I meticulously monitored my public interactions with him.

Nikki, one of my classmates at UMass, became instrumental in my personal and professional life. Nikki and I became best of friends during the first year of the program. We helped one another academically while pulling all-nighters, and working nonstop upon complex projects and case studies together. However, as year two progressed in the program, my heart grew tired of the constant hide and seek game I played with Jake. I told Nikki I had to share something with her.

"Nikki, I'm not fully happy. Part of me feels entrapped and constantly in a lie with those around me."

"What do you mean?" she asked.

"I hate not being myself. I constantly fear other's opinions and judgments cast upon me."

I looked over at her. Saying the words still greatly troubled me. I wished she just understood me without actually having to utter the words.

"Is there something you need to tell me?" she asked.

I looked down at the ground.

"I'm gay, Nikki. Jake isn't my friend, he's actually my boyfriend."

Without hesitation she responded,

"Well, you've got to do whatever makes you happy. You only live one life, so as long as you're happy, I'm happy for you."

We hugged, even though she's not a fan of hugging. I thanked her immensely for her support. Our friendship exponentially grew after my revelation. Nikki encouraged my happiness at all costs. She challenged my decision to hide Jake's importance in my life when he visited. A couple of months later, he returned to town. We attended a small gathering with a few of my friends from school. I worked up some courage, and approached one of my friends.

"Hi Karen, this is my boyfriend, Jake," I confidently said.

"Nice to meet you, Jake!" she replied.

We chatted, and then walked away. My uneasy feelings reminded me of my awkward and insecure teenage days. I wondered what Karen would tell my other friends. Nikki walked over and interrupted my internal worries and thoughts.

"How'd it go?" she asked.

"Good...I think. I casually introduced him as my boyfriend and she seemed to be just fine with it."

"Good job," she replied. "Now get over it. Go grab a drink and be happy."

We ran into a few more of my friends as the evening progressed. The words felt just as strange coming from my lips as they did the first time. Again, I repeated my introduction. I feared the worst. Nothing happened. I introduced someone as my boyfriend for the first time in my life, and it felt damn good.

Jake and I had a long conversation that evening. He thanked me from the bottom of his heart for revealing our relationship to my classmates at school. I revealed myself to a small group of strangers. It wasn't the most difficult crowd to tell, but still acted to shed back yet another layer of my insecurities. Then, the inevitable question soon followed. Jake asked,

"Just when are we going to be ourselves when we visit your hometown?"

He expressed feelings of hurt when I disguised him to my hometown family and friends. Jake wanted us to get to the next level of comfort. I expressed my hesitations.

"My extended family and hometown friends have known me as 'straight' for as long as they've known me. I'm not quite sure I'm ready to unbury my secret to everyone in my life just yet."

"When is the right time?" he asked. "I felt so hidden when I met your relatives, and hate going back and forth faking that we're just friends all the time."

I empathized and agreed. I then turned the tables on him.

"I've made some progress since we've started dating. I told my best friend at school, and now introduced you to some of my other classmates as well. You still haven't even told your parents or any of your friends about you, or about us. How do you think that makes me feel?"

Jake pondered the words. He convincingly stated that his family would disown him. I walked him through my story in depth, my similar fears, and my outcome with my parents and sister. He expressed certainty that his family wouldn't understand. We looked at one another, and knew that we had to change something. We shared this conversation many times before. It started to affect the health of our relationship. Visiting my hometown meant visiting with two separate personalities. Visiting his hometown was entirely out of the question.

Coming Out to Family and Friends

My head spun out of control. I cared for Jake deeply, but my stomach felt completely nauseous at the thought of telling my extended family and friends. Anti-gay messages rushed through my head from my aunts and uncles. I recalled my high school friends routinely throwing the word "fag" and "gay" around, and the feelings of never wanting them to know about me. I worried about my family's reputation in our hometown.

I didn't want my family and friends to slowly find out about me or to hear it through the grapevine, either. I wanted them to hear it directly from me, and I wanted to just rip the Band-Aid right off. I forced myself to understand the importance of no longer feeling inferior to others. No more tiptoeing around. Take me or leave me. It was finally time to set myself free. In early 2011, on the verge of my 26th birthday, I worked up the courage to send the following email to my aunts, uncles, cousins, and closest childhood and high school friends:

"My beloved family and friends,

I have come to a stage in my life where I am no longer comfortable hiding under my own skin. I have been through a lot over the course of my young life, and most of it was internalized and hidden. Why? Because I was "different." I am gay. It's something that I've known since I was much younger, but have hidden because it was so painful to think that I was different, that something was wrong with me, and that society would forever judge who I am as a person.

I spent countless nights crying myself to sleep, and praying for God to change me and make me "normal" like the people around me. I went through years of silent suffering, trying to change my natural being at its very core. But I am who I am, and I'm finally able to free myself from the fears of what society, and others, may think of me. As long as it's taken to finally be ok with myself to tell others, it's something that I have to do for me. I told my parents and sister and they've loved me just the same. I am the same person, the same Adam as I have always been; it's just that something may now change in your minds or perceptions about me.

I am so very strong in my faith, and the amazing relationship with my God that I have. I know that this is how I was created, and that God would not expect me to spend a life trying to hide or lie about who I am. Who I was made to be. I have spent enough time doing this, and the time is finally over.

Unfortunately, one of my fears has always been that people would forever view me differently, or not accept me for who I am. As much as I love each and every one of you, if you choose not to love me or accept me, that's something that I can't help. That is no longer stopping me from being comfortable in my own skin.

I have been writing a book about growing up as a gay Christian, and wanted to come out that way – but the time is now. I am very happy with myself and with who I am. This is perhaps the

most important thing I have ever done in my life…liberating myself. I love you all so very much. I am so amazed at the incredible and loving family and friends that God has blessed me with.
Sincerely (and still just the same ol' me),
Adam"

After sending that email, I had no clue what responses I would receive, if any at all. I called my parents and told them what I had done. My Dad replied, "I'm proud of you son. You're finally becoming like me…because you've grown some balls!" After a brief discussion, I sensed the next question before it came. "Just when are you going to tell your Grandmother, Adam?" they asked.

My Grandma didn't use email. Even if she did, that type of communication wouldn't have been appropriate. She loved me deeply and spoiled me my entire life. I had to call her. My Grandma, a devout Roman Catholic, went to church every week. I never even heard the word gay or lesbian come out of her mouth. I had no clue where she stood on the issue. The large generation gap intimidated me. I placed a very heavy expectation on myself to try and be a good grandchild, and live up to my grandparent's wishes for success in my life.

With my Grandpa no longer around, speaking to my Grandma seemed symbolic of speaking to both of them. They did everything together, and shared very similar beliefs on many of the same issues. I took in a deep breath, and rehearsed what to say. My fingers refused to dial the numbers. I placed my hands on the table to calm them down from shaking. I rehearsed again.

The call began. My memory completely blanked on what I had planned to say. Upon hearing my Grandma's voice, I immediately started to cry. Her voice filled with concern. She asked, "What's wrong my Adam?"

Attempting to gather myself, I asked,

"Would you love me no matter what Grandma?"

"Of course, honey," she replied.

I stalled. I looked around my room neurotically and tapped the phone against my head, squeezing my eyes shut. I opened my eyes. Again, my mind drew a complete blank on what to say.

"Grandma, I'm gay."

I absolutely lost it. My Grandma began to cry as well. Hearing my Grandma cry made me even sadder. My apprehension grew with the passing of each moment. Neither one of us spoke for 30 seconds. I wiped my tears and stared at the ceiling in my room.

"As long as you're happy, honey," she faintly replied.

Completely stunned, I couldn't initially reply. My tightly clenched hands opened up. Shaking my head in disbelief, I said, "What?"

She sniffled and repeated the sentiment. It absolutely blew me away. Her unfailing, unwavering, and unconditional love for me made me speechless. As one of the people I feared most in my life of telling, she instantly alleviated my fears. We cried for a minute, and my Grandma then asked a few questions. Her concerns weren't about me being gay. She made sure that I was happy, and told me to remain a good kid with a good heart. I assured her that I would.

My Grandma's initial and genuine response reminded me that this was not for anyone else, but myself. My happiness. It seemed selfish to me to think like that, but it was. I needed to grab hold of my own life and happiness. Surely, nobody would just hand it over to me on a silver platter.

Certain family members never replied to my email, nor did they ever bring it up via phone or in person. It didn't bother me much. I took their silence as a pretty straightforward "I don't agree with you" response. However, over the next few days, the majority of my family and friend's responses poured in.

My Aunt Kathy wrote:

"Dear 'Same Ol' Adam'…

Thank you so much for your honesty and brave heart! I feel so very sad that for all these years, you have been hiding and didn't feel that you could have shared this with the closest people in your life. I hope we did not make you feel uncomfortable over those painful years, for any reason, but especially this! If we did, I am very sorry for that and ask for your forgiveness. We love you now as we have always…nothing will ever change that, you know that.

To have had to feel different or that something was wrong with you had to be so painful…no one wants to feel like that! To judge is not up to us as humans…that is for God the Creator of ALL things. It is not up to anyone to judge another human being, even though we do it all the time, usually daily. If you feel as you say, "normal" and now free from that fear, than we are happy for you

Adam. We would rather have you be honest and live the way you choose to live, than to continue to hide behind a lie. You are right, God would not want you to continue to live a lie, in fact He says, "do not lie," so in that way, you are being faithful to Him and to yourself and to all of those who love you.

To live and to laugh and especially Adam, to LOVE…that is the greatest thing that God created. Our hearts and our souls and the ability to love and show compassion to one another…that is the greatest gift from above.
Talk soon, Love you Adam…ALWAYS!! Ciao!"

My Aunt Carol wrote:

"We love you, as we always have, unconditionally! Nothing you are will take our love from you because of your sexual preferences, silly boy…You were born Adam, our nephew, our blood, our family, and you are loved naturally. We absolutely love you and always will! End of Story!!!"

My Aunt Annie wrote:

"I love love love you!!!! Jesus came to save us, not to condemn us. How amazing you are always to this world!!!! You are a beacon of light in a dark world!"

Stevan, my childhood best friend, shared:

"Adam, I wish you told me earlier, you know I would have had absolutely no problem with it. You've been my best friend and brother for over 20 years, and this changes absolutely nothing. The only thing that upsets me is knowing that you had to hide and deal with this all on your own, without much help. I'm sorry you've had to do it on your own, but I'm glad that's finally over!

I can't imagine how hard it's been, that must have been such a huge burden and weight on you. I can imagine telling your "religious" family and cousins must be daunting, but they all love you and I doubt would react any differently than I have. But if so, then screw them!

Don't for one second think this changes anything…I will still need to approve of anyone that you date. I am just glad that you were finally able to tell me and I just wanted to let you know this changes absolutely…and I mean absolutely…nothing about us. I'll talk to you soon and I'm glad everything is going well!
Love ya, Stevan"

Then came the jokester, my Aunt Jeannie:

"WELL SHIT!! TELL ME SOMETHING I DIDN'T KNOW, IS THAT IT?? I first suspected it when I saw you come downstairs in a pink tutu when you were a little boy – yes, I knew it then – and I didn't even hope you would change one bit! Seriously, I'm soooo glad you're "out" – of course you were under great stress all these years but now you can relax…aren't you glad you don't have to hide?

Thank God for 2011 – and for all the people before you who paved the way for you! Life will still be hard for you, but as long as

you believe in yourself, are a good human being, and treat others likewise, you'll be honky dory nephew! So, go back to your life, be happy, make others happy, and piss on the rest of them!
Love you always, Aunt Jeannie"

My Grandpa George said:
"Well I wouldn't call this good news, but I'm happy for you. Keep living your good life. I love you."

My cousin Mathieu wrote:

"Adam, I love you, and I'm so proud to have you in our family. Just wanted to say how much respect I have for what you did. You're a strong dude, and it must feel great to no longer live in fear of what other people think of you. We love you just the same as ever. I know some of our very religious family will give you kickback, but truly, without any disrespect to them, I think they are immature. Immature that they haven't understood the biggest lesson of all in life: God loves all people, and we are here to love, help, and support one another. That is life. We are here to make the world a better place, and to love everyone just the same. You can't get taught that, you just have to get it. I get it. I know many people in our family do too. But for those that don't, I can only hope that one day they will. But don't let that hold you back. You are awesome man, you've got a great heart, and we're all so proud of you. Anyways, love ya man and stay strong!"

My cousin Gina followed by saying:

"Hi cuz…thank you so much for the beautiful email…it means so much that you trust us enough to let us in a little bit deeper into your life! I am confident that no one of importance would ever judge you…judgment in my opinion stems from ignorance. Ever since my Dad passed away unexpectedly, I've realized how short life is, and you only live once. Why not spend that once chance, that one opportunity, being happy with yourself? I am very proud of your strength, and I wish you the best! I am so happy for you!"

I received additional phone calls and texts from my extremely supportive cousins like Jamie, Miles, Tyler, Nina and Greg, close friends, and family members like my Aunt Teresa and my loving "second Mom" Sue. The amount of support overwhelmed me a bit, in a good way. My family and friend's responses made me incredibly thankful to have so many loving people in my immediate life. It inspired me to hear words of encouragement from multiple family members raised to reflect a different belief of what they expressed to me.

Jake also revealed his sexuality and his relationship status to his parents and siblings. He didn't experience the same support. His siblings challenged him to question the 'decisions' that he made. His parents didn't want to believe him. They warned him of the strict repercussions that he would face accordingly to the Bible. They isolated him. Upon hearing this disturbing news, I immediately flashed back to Kevin. I feared the same internal battle and anguish from Jake. Jake, however, handled the situation differently. He owned his intellectual and economical independence, and stuck with our relationship. He put a wall up in regards to his family's opinions. He didn't express his hurt to me, but I could tell that it affected him deeply. There were days that a family memory popped up, and Jake fell into a complete daze and blank stare, unable to converse. His parents no longer called him on holidays, and they seldom replied to his text messages. I shook my head in utter disbelief of their actions. I grew resentment towards them even though I never met them.

Unwelcomed

In 2010, The ELCA made national news when they allowed ordination of LGBT Ministers and Pastors in their churches. I desired to find an LGBT-friendly church, and set out on a mission to join a worship team as well. I visited a few local churches around UMass. I found a non-denominational Christian church not too far from my apartment that had a contemporary band and a small choir. I attended the church for a couple of Sundays before inquiring about joining. After service, I approached the Pastor and asked if I could speak with him. We walked around a short hallway and into his office. He politely offered for me to take a seat.

"I'm fairly new to the area and I've been looking to find a church that I could regularly attend," I said. "I'm excited to have found your church."

"That's terrific!" he proclaimed.

"I would also like to inquire about joining the band and worship team here, if you would consider me."

His eyes lit up. He squeezed his hands together and said,

"That's great news! We are always looking for youth to join our worship team. We would love to have you join!"

It could have, and perhaps should have, ended there. And up to that point in my life, it had always ended there. But for some reason, it wasn't enough for me this time around. I needed to be myself and be accepted for my true self. My knee slowly bounced up and down as my mind became engrossed with thoughts of honesty. I thought to myself, "I sang for years in Siena's choir and not a soul there knew that I was gay, so…what did it matter? Did it matter if the voice I sang with came from white or black skin, male or female, or a gay or straight person? No. I sang with a voice to worship God. Why does this matter to me now?"

After having progressively reached different levels of comfort with myself, it did matter. I didn't want to leave the room until I said it. I needed to know that I would be accepted for who I was, wholly and entirely. Nerves ran rampant through my body at the thought of coming out to a religious leader. I silenced them. Trusting my gut, I proceeded.

"Pastor, I want to let you know something before you fully accept me joining your church or worship team. I've struggled with accepting it my entire life, but in the last couple of years, I have really come to terms with myself and have started to fully accept who I am, and who I was made to be. I have come to know God as a gracious and loving God, one who created me to be the exact man that I have become. Pastor, I…am gay. I have always known that I was gay, and always will be gay. It is not a decision, nor does it define my life on a day-to-day basis, no more so than a straight person is not solely defined by their sexuality. It is simply one part of me. I want to be honest and straightforward in letting you know this, as to not be surprised if it ever came out down the road."

He took in a deep breath. With slight hesitation and caution surrounding his words, he slowly began to formulate a reply.

"Adam…first of all, thank you for sharing that with me. I know just how difficult it must be to share a lifelong struggle with a stranger, and for that I do thank you."

He paused. He placed his hands together in his lap and moved his eyes from the ground up towards me.

"As difficult as it must have been for you to go through your struggles, I just don't think that having a gay member of our worship team would send a good message to the rest of the team, and to the church. Unfortunately, I would not be able to extend the offer to become a member of our team and church, unless you would agree to pray with me over this issue. But, it sounds like you've already made up your mind on that."

I looked at him as I slowly raised my eyebrows. I bit my bottom lip and said, "Well Pastor, I do thank you for your time."

I did my best to fake a smile and I shook his hand goodbye. Part of me wanted to turn around and sarcastically proclaim, "Just kidding, I'm straight!" and see if he would have re-accepted me back into the church. I continued walking, and digested the message that I just received.

I firmly held onto my identity as I walked away. But when I reached the end of the hall and opened up the doors to the outside, my mind spiraled. Certain insecurities weren't completely and easily avoidable. The topic spanned many years and contained so many painful memories behind it. It deeply troubled me to hear firsthand, "You are not welcomed here" and to be asked to "pray the gay" out of me. Pastors and Priests are called by God to aid in delivering God's message to people on this earth. Was this message from God, or was it just from a man mistaken in his interpretation?

I got behind the wheel of my Jeep and sat in silence. I fidgeted with the service's handout, which I still held onto with my left hand. I looked through the day's message: love and peace with one another, and finding joy in the Lord. I couldn't have felt any farther from the sermon's meaning. I shook my head at the dissonance I experienced. I tapped the paper against the door of my car and eventually crumbled it up. My hopes deflated. I shot myself in the foot with my own honestly.

My mind wrestled over the issue for the remainder of the day. Coming out to a religious leader took a lot of thoughts, energy, and courage. The last thing I wanted to do was to go through the process again, after receiving his response. My long standing insecurities and self-doubt battled my newfound confidence. Ironically, in an attempt to step closer to God, I got pushed away. I found myself not attending church after that for quite some time. I certainly never returned to that church again.

Homosexuality in the Bible

I pushed myself to further understand the issues surrounding homosexuality and Christianity. I needed to completely educate myself on this deeply debated, misunderstood, and misconstrued topic. How many prejudices, misconceptions, fears and attitudes stem from our own cultural beliefs, and how many actually stem from the Bible itself? I took to the Bible as a scholar through study and prayer, and read several books and countless articles to form an educated opinion on the topic. Identifying as a gay Christian sparked my interest in such research and understanding, and demanded my ability to answer the question, "How can you identify as both?"

The Bible is broken into two main sections: the Old Testament and the New Testament. The Old Testament books are known as the books of the Law, which regulated almost every aspect of Hebrew (Jewish people's) lives. From the Old Testament, it is shown that God creates, loves, and sustains all of His creation, and also provides us with the Ten Commandments and other strict rules and laws at the time of the Israelites. It also discusses the Hebrew prophets foreseeing the coming of a Messiah or a King. The New Testament tells us the story of Jesus' birth, life, ministry, death, and resurrection. Although unknown and not believed by many at the time of His life, Jesus proved to be the Messiah (or the Christ) and thus Christianity was born after His death and subsequent resurrection. The greatest two commandments according to Jesus' teaching were the love of God and the love of other people.

Amidst my research and study regarding what the Bible actually says about homosexuality, one thing became very clear to me. Christians who strictly oppose homosexuality selectively choose which verses to use to back up this stance. These verses are taken completely out of context, and are interpreted literally. These same Christians disregard countless other verses and themes throughout the Bible, and do not take them literally. By taking some verses literally and others not, this method makes religion a personal preference and decision-making process. Cultural and personal discriminations become justified wherever a person sees fit. This ambiguous and hypocritical approach wasn't enough for me. I dug deep into the history and context of the passages in question.

Throughout history, people have misconstrued and misused the Bible to satisfy their own personal beliefs and prejudices. The Bible has been utilized to justify some of the worst atrocities ever committed on our planet. Hitler used the Bible to justify his execution of six million Jews during World War II, as have many others who have led brutal genocides around the world. In the U.S., the Bible was used to justify slavery, child abuse, as well as the Ku Klux Klan's main mission. The Bible has been used to justify sexism and the oppression of women pretty much since the beginning of time. In all of these instances, direct quotes from the Bible were utilized to "back up" these leaders and stances. People divorced passages entirely from their context to show God's support of racism, sexism, slavery, and genocide and war throughout our history. Some Christians still provide the same injustice and false teachings to my LGBT brothers and sisters.

Many people do not even know the history of the word 'homosexual' or how it came to exist within the Bible. The word homosexual first came to existence in 1869 when Karl Benkert, a Hungarian journalist created the term by combining the "homo" (Greek word for 'same'), with the Latin word 'sexual'.[2] He campaigned for human rights after one of his gay friends killed himself for being blackmailed due to his sexuality.

For the first time in history in 1958, a person translating a Bible into English decided that certain words meant "homosexual," even though there was no such word in the Greek or Hebrew languages at the time the Bible was written. No similar translation for such existed.[3] The Bible has been translated from Hebrew and Aramaic to Greek, then to Latin, and finally to English. The researchers, Pastors, and Professors that have studied the Bible, amidst their mastery of these languages and contexts, still have large debates on how certain words and phrases were translated into modern day English.

For example, the original Greek word of "arsenokoitai" has been translated by Greek scholars to mean "male prostitutes." Various Biblical translations such as the King James Version use "abusers of themselves with mankind," whereas the English Standard Version uses the term "homosexuals." The discrepancies amongst our own Bibles and their various translations become apparent. Can a word with a completely different meaning and understanding, formed in 1869 and placed into the Bible in 1958, be all-encompassing of what the authors wrote about in other languages thousands of years ago?

Homosexuality as it is understood today, consenting and caring partners that choose to enter into a loving relationship, is entirely different to what passages exist in the Bible regarding such. The few passages in the Bible that some pertain to include all of homosexuality suggest abusive behavior, rape, and idolatry among other sins. These themes are very far from what is now understand of homosexuality. Yet, in some churches and Christian cultures, homosexuality is placed under an umbrella term evolving into purely negative and unacceptable implications.

As my mind, understanding, and education levels all expanded, I realized that I couldn't take the statement "being gay is a sin" as a fact. I couldn't rely upon the country's cultural and personal prejudices against LGBT people without having a solid understanding of the passages in the Bible myself. After all, even though around 80% of Americans identify as being Christians,[4] the statistics on American's knowledge of the Bible is astounding. More than 60% of Americans cannot name either the four Gospels of the New Testament, or half of the Ten Commandments.[5] Even further yet, a core teaching of the entire Christian faith is the sinless nature and perfection of Jesus during his time on earth. A 2009 study showed that more than one-fifth of American Christians (22%)

'strongly agreed' that Jesus sinned during his time on earth, and an additional 17% 'agreed somewhat' to the statement.[6] If almost 40% of Americans who identify as Christian don't even understand a core pillar of the faith that they self-identify under, how then can I entrust them to correctly educate me on the correct understanding and context of a select few passages?

Amidst my research, I discovered that homosexuality (as it is understood today) was not addressed nor written about during the time that the Bible was written. The references to homosexuality in the Bible mainly refer to the prostitution of young boys, and the rape of enslavement of prisoners by male soldiers used as mechanisms of power thousands of years ago. In fact, when reading and studying the few passages and their context which the Bible refers to as "homosexual practices," I discovered that they are mainly referring to violating other Bible prohibitions including the aforementioned themes of rape, prostitution, and idolatry.

Although some Christians use the Bible to justify their anti-gay stance from a few passages that are interpreted literally, so many other quotes from the Bible are completed disregarded. If people utilized this same methodology of using Biblical quotes to back-up their stance and discrimination on homosexuality, why then is the same literal interpretation not used to justify the following passages pertaining to sex:

> Deuteronomy 22:13-21: If a bride is found not to be a virgin, the Bible demands that she be executed on the spot by stoning.

Deuteronomy 22:22: If a married person has sex with someone else's husband or wife, the Bible commands that both adulterers be stoned to death.

Mark 10:1-12: Divorce is strictly forbidden by the Bible in both testaments, as is remarriage by divorcees.

Mark 12:18-27: When a man died childless, his widow is ordered by Biblical law to have intercourse with each of his brothers in turn until she bears her deceased husband a male heir.

There are many practices that are not agree upon within the Bible's teaching of sex, including: sex with a prostitute is acceptable for husbands but not for wives; slavery and sex with slaves is acceptable; marriage for girls ages 11-13 is acceptable; inter-racial marriage is not acceptable; discussing or even naming a sexual organ is not acceptable; and the list goes on and on.[7] Hitler, the KKK, slave owners, child abusers, and women oppressors all did just that. They picked apart the Bible and utilized scripture to justify their own prejudices and objectives. As William Shakespeare once said, "Even the Devil can cite scripture for his purpose."

However, when Jesus came to the earth, He taught that certain commands in the Bible are no longer appropriate for our lives, or are just. Above all else, Jesus taught to love and to accept one another, and that no one has the right to judge or condemn others. He strictly warns that God and God alone is the only judge. He taught us that we must use reason, love, humility, and acceptance in our lives. If we interpreted every single passage and word literally as written (or as translated into modern day newly created words) we would be in a very poor, unhealthy, and unsafe state as Christians. We would still be stuck in the times with a complete disregard for science, facts, and modern day understood truths and research.

When Galileo first defended his research and studies relating to heliocentrism (the belief that the earth and planets revolve around the Sun), he experienced a large backlash from political and religious leaders in Italy. Leaders used quotes directly from the Bible to condemn his work and to accuse him of going against God's holy word. Although Galileo provided proof of his studies and work, he was officially brought to trial in 1633. Galileo was sentenced and found "vehemently suspect of heresy, namely of having held the opinions that the Sun lies motionless at the centre of the universe... after it has been declared contrary to Holy Scripture." He was required to "adjure, curse and detest" those opinions.[8] Furthermore, Galileo was sentenced to life imprisonment in his own home, where he remained for the rest of his days. Yet, years later, his claims and studies were found to be exactly true. Galileo followed the Augustinian position that Biblical texts need not be interpreted literally, if a literal interpretation contradicts science and our God-given gift of reasoning.[9]

Along this same regard, how can we disregard all current research in regards to what we have now come to refer to as homosexuality? How can we ignore the largest health organizations in the United States, the brightest doctors, psychologists and researchers that have concluded that homosexuality is an innate, natural part of us as human beings? According to the American Psychological Association (APA) they do not consider sexual orientation to be a conscious choice that can be voluntarily changed.[10] The detrimental, unhealthy, and psychologically disturbing "conversion therapies" which include shock therapy, reparative therapy, praying the gay away, and every other absurd attempt to change someone's sexuality has been ruled as neither safe nor effective by the APA, along with all other major health and science organizations across the country.

If we believe in scientific discoveries such as treatments and surgeries for cancer and diseases, immunizations that have eradicated diseases and plagues, the sun being at the center of our universe, and countless others, why are some people then able to dismiss decades of research and understanding into homosexuality as it is understood today? How can Christians condemn LGBT people, and then completely disregard other groups of people and actions just as specifically called out in the Bible?

Unfortunately, as per a theme throughout the history of mankind, people like to cherry-pick which things to abide by and which to disregard. Beliefs are justified in order to align with personal biases. These actions do not represent Christianity. To condemn and to judge is not living out a life filled with Christ. Hacking apart the Bible to justify prejudices only guarantees the many mistakes made throughout our world's history continue to be repeated.

To follow what Jesus taught us, we must not allow hindrance from personal and cultural discriminations and prejudices that are strongly held against the LGBT community. We must challenge ourselves to study, understand, and interpret Biblical passages for their content and context, as they were written at the time. We must learn from our past, and from those that have so atrociously misused Biblical texts and passages to justify their own harmful intentions and prejudices. Homosexuality as it is understood today, as an innate, natural part of human beings with consensually loving and dedicated relationships, is very far removed from Biblical references from thousands of years ago when so many cruelties happened and war, greed, slavery, and rape were commonplace.

I know deep within my heart that God loves me, accepts me as His child, and expects me to treat all of those around me with that same love and acceptance, free of judgment. Throughout my life, I have seen hypocrisy run rampant through Christian churches and belief systems. It is unfortunately these same people that turn people *away* from God. I know that I am doing the best with the tool-kit, power of my mind, and the love that I have been blessed with by God. I take it personally to live out my life as Jesus instructed, to love others and to serve a life of absolute inclusion. Not once in Jesus' life did he exclude any single person, group, or minority. I'm shocked and saddened by people who identify themselves as Christians, spending their lives trying to educate others to exclude certain groups from their churches, homes, and societal laws.

Joseph Goebbels, Hitler's Propaganda Minister once said, "If you tell a lie big enough and keep repeating it, people will eventually come to believe it."[11]

I once believed the lies. I adopted the stance that homosexuality was wrong even before my adolescent sexuality and hormones began to kick in. Without the proper study and education surrounding any topic in the Bible, personal and cultural prejudices, biases, beliefs, and discriminations unfortunately prevail ahead of God's meaning and purpose for our lives. We were created to love God and to love one another. Don't let anyone's misconstrued message of God affect you and your personal faith, religion, spirituality, or belief that you were created anything less than perfect just the way you are.

Venturing into Healthcare and Colorado

During my first year and a half at UMass, I adamantly researched PhD programs in business. Alongside my close friendship with Deb, my work under multiple Professors at UMass furthered my interest in pursuing a career in higher education. I attended dissertation defenses, spoke with admissions counselors from various schools, and helped teach undergraduate classes. One day, reality smacked me upside the head. If my heart wasn't 100% dedicated towards it, I wouldn't make it through the four to five additional years of intensive studying, researching, and writing. I forfeit the career path I once thought so confidently that I would pursue.

My life's course became once again unknown. I watched my classmates narrow down their interests to specific jobs and careers. On the contrary, I felt like a leaf being blown around in the wind. My interest and excitement aligned with many things, and I picked up things fairly quickly. But before I rested in one place for too long, the wind picked right back up and carried me off to a new adventure.

At UMass, I worked under Professor Cortez during my second year of study. Uniquely, Professor Cortez served as my first ever gay mentor. Her successful long-term relationship inspired me. She was gay, successful, and truly happy, and it encouraged me to aim for the same in my life. I looked towards her for advice after arriving back at square one with my career prospects.

"You need to refocus your thinking," she said. "Life's path is a journey, not a destination. If you think of it as a destination, you'll always feel that you've never reached it. It's the journey in life that makes it fun."

I smiled and slightly nodded my head. Her calming presence and approach put me at ease. She continued, "Some people may seem to have control of their parachutes in life, and appear to control their landing. Perhaps you don't have a parachute, but rather a canopy to fly with."

She held out both of her arms and tilted her body side to side.

"Do you know those flying canopies people hold out with their arms?" she asked.

"Yes, I do."

"This canopy still allows for you to land, but perhaps the wind changes your course more easily than others. Your destination may take longer to reach, but your journey will be filled with excitement. Life always has a way of working itself out."

In the following weeks, I bounced ideas off of Professor Cortez, and kept my mind open to various industries. When we passed one another in the halls, she would hold out her arms to symbolize my flying canopy. During my last semester at UMass, I landed an externship with one of New England's largest private health insurance companies. Subsequently, it sparked my interest in the healthcare industry. Professor Cortez encouraged me to pursue it.

One of the Professors in my MBA program regularly published within the industry and worked with many large systems across the country. I scheduled a meeting with him to pick his brain and to discuss a potential career and future within healthcare. Eager to hear his advice, expertise on the subject, and opinions on breaking into the field, I walked into his office.

Awards and honors decorated his office walls with his many accomplishments. He sat behind a cluttered desk. I sat down, and explained my interest. I displayed a few printed job descriptions in the healthcare field that I hoped to qualify for. I placed my resume on his desk so that he could view my academic and professional experiences. He slowly leaned back in his large black leather chair. He blankly stared towards me. Without looking at the documents that I placed near him for discussion, he squinted his eyes and shook his head in disbelief.

"What the hell do you know about healthcare?" he said, glaring at me from across the desk.

My excitement deflated. I attempted my best to not let his lackluster response discourage me, but my confusion trumped my will to persist. He fiddled with his planner, and made it clear that he had other things on his busy day's agenda. I walked back to my apartment with my seemingly non-impressive resume in hand. I felt like an idiotic dreamer with my head in the clouds.

The following morning, I woke up full of ambition. His response fueled my determination to prove him wrong. I set out on my own journey to network my way into the industry.

My fellow classmates scrambled to find jobs. I scrambled to network. I meticulously researched companies all across the states I desired to live in: New York, Massachusetts, and Colorado. I researched company's missions, visions and values, and chose organizations that appealed to me. I reached out to human resources teams and worked my way up to recruiters and operational contacts. I set up lunches, informal meetings, and calls with representatives from various companies. I also networked with UMass alumni that worked in healthcare.

A month after graduation, I received a telephone call. One of the gentlemen I met with passed along my information to a few of his contacts. My resume surfaced for a business manager position in private practice in the Boston area. The owners of these practices, two Doctors, reached out to set up an interview. A few days after my interview, I received an official offer with an immediate start date. I got my life in order and quickly moved out to Boston.

I managed twenty people at two practices, and learned the industry as quickly as I could. My emails, texts, and calls started each morning around 6:00am, and finally stopped around 10:00pm each evening. My free time quickly belonged to the Doctors, weekends included. Six months into the job, I learned some troubling news. The IRS audited my boss for years of suspected tax evasion. He obstructed the investigation, making matters worse and raising many red flags. I became increasingly put in charge of their finances and operations of their practices. They gave me an attractive raise. I knew that I had to flee from the position quickly. I didn't want to get my hands muddied in those waters.

My boss attended multiple hearings in court, and awaited his sentence. I searched for other jobs. Simultaneously, a human resource specialist whom I had networked with in Colorado reached out to me. She considered me for an open position, and wanted me to fly out for an interview. A week later, I received my first ever job offer in Colorado. I finally had the chance to move closer to my sister, and to live with my long-distance boyfriend Jake whom I only saw but a few times a year. I turned in my two weeks notice in Boston. My boss received his prison sentence. I moved to Colorado right after Thanksgiving of 2011. The state's characteristically bright sunshine welcomed me upon my arrival. I began my journey in a new state with a new job, and lived with a boyfriend for the very first time in my life.

Stepping out on a Limb That Broke

Jake didn't care to socialize as much as I did. He often stayed home while I ventured off to explore much of my new home state's surroundings with Tiffany. A few months after my move to Colorado, St. Patrick's Day 2012 approached. I planned to spend the day with Tiffany, and we looked forward to it for weeks. She bought hats, beads, shirts, and noisemakers in anticipation for the day's festivities. Much to her dismay, Tiffany came down with a bad stomach bug in the days leading up to St. Patty's.

Though she couldn't attend, Tiffany still encouraged me to get my first experience of the holiday in Denver. I navigated my way down to the city, and arrived at one of the many crowded bars with people decked out in green. I grabbed a beer and socialized with a few people. Cindy, a girl around my age, introduced me to a few of her friends. Cindy's friend Glen handed me a pair of lit green glasses. The other girls placed gold and green beads around my neck. The friendly group invited me to join them in their pub crawl, and we left the noisy and overly crowded bar to head to another.

Beads and green boas flew everywhere on the closed off streets. People carried their stumbling drunken friends, though it hadn't yet reached noon. We stopped at a couple of bars, and Cindy and her friends genuinely welcomed me into their group with drinks and conversation. The drinks continued to flow, and day soon turned into night. Cindy inquired whether or not I had a girlfriend. I fended off her question with a smile while looking away, and casually replied, "No, I do not." She draped her arm around my shoulder and made a toast to new friendships. I clinked my beer glass with hers, along with Glen's and the other members of our group. Before letting go of my shoulder, Cindy leaned over and pressed the side of her face up against mine. I worried that she liked me, and wrestled back and forth with thoughts of whether or not to reveal my sexuality.

Introducing myself to complete strangers with full honesty proved challenging. I still withheld my secret from immediate strangers in my life and in the workplace setting. Part of me still felt uneasy and self-conscious about being gay around those I didn't know. Part of me still felt inferior.

A few of the girls in the group became persistent with the question. "So, do you have a girlfriend or not?" they asked, smiling through their words. I repeated that I did not.

My mind challenged itself. Why not just go for it? Why not just tell them the truth? Cindy raised her eyebrows at me and winked. She leaned in close to me and repeated the inquiry.

"So," she said, "you don't have a girlfriend, huh?"

"No, I'm gay," I said.

"You're kidding me, right?"

"I am not."

Her humor and flirtatious gestures immediately disappeared. A look of judgment formed in her eyes that made me feel less than a person. Her smile turned into a grim expression. Her body language changed from warm and welcoming to cold and completely closed off. Cindy folded her arms, and took a step away from me. I immediately thought, "Why did I tell her? Why didn't I just do what I always had done, and not bring it up?"

Cindy blatantly whispered what I said to her friends. One by one, they shared the news with each other. Their expressions soon matched Cindy's. Glen glared at me with a look of disgust, and immediately turned his back to me. Another girl in the group began referring to me as "gay boy." I instantly felt shunned upon and not accepted. They slowly moved a few feet down the bar. I remained where I stood.

In one brief statement and revelation, my status transformed from newfound friend to complete outcast. They exiled me. "Gay boy" in particular kept echoing in my mind. I felt so lame for letting their statements and judgments affect me. I tried to convince myself that it doesn't matter what other people thought. It didn't work. It hurt to be completely rejected by a group of people and made to feel lesser as a person. I placed my unfinished beer on the counter, and left the bar alone. I fought back tears while walking down the street, a few of which managed to sneak down my face. I quickly wiped them away with the back of my hand.

I called Tiffany. Although she felt very ill, I didn't know where else to turn. I needed my big sister. Tiffany became infuriated and outraged. "Just wait until I get my hands on them," she said.

In between my emotional statements of "Tiff, it's ok." And, "Don't worry about it, I'll be fine," I heard her getting dressed. She prepared to go downtown and make some heads roll. I encouraged her to not risk getting sicker and to remain at home. She never let anyone mess with me growing up, and this situation wasn't any different. After five minutes of attempting to convince her, I finally calmed her down.

She listened to everything I shared. She found a way to make me laugh. She walked me through the milestones I made in my personal life, and challenged me not to give up now. I reflected upon the fact that I still fell short of fully owning my identity, after allowing the interaction to affect me so deeply.

I made my way home, but not before finishing up one of the most supportive and loving conversations of my life. Tiffany inundated my phone with texts and calls for days on end, reminding me just how much she loved and cared for me.

In the following week, my feelings of dejection became compounded by feelings of disappointment. The group's response disappointed me, but so did mine. I let their judgments and laughter hurt and affect me. I still maintained ghosts in my closet that controlled certain lifelong fears. I needed to let other people's perceptions and opinions roll right off of me and not think twice about them. I demanded to be in my own driver's seat in life and to no longer let others control me. I determined to remove negativity, more so the fear of negativity, from my life.

Tackling the Business World as a Gay Man

The professional front remained the largest void in my life in regards to my own comfort and acceptance. Even after coming out to my family and friends, I still thought I might never come out in the business world. I feared discrimination. I read stories of LGBT people getting fired for coming out at work. I didn't want to cause any potential disruption, or risk putting my job or myself in a vulnerable position. I felt most content and most protected by limiting the secret information to those in my personal life.

Two years after moving to Colorado, I landed a new job. My responsibilities grew. My honesty in the workplace didn't. The first two weeks of work passed in my new role. I received the all-too-familiar questions. Many of my new coworkers asked, "Are you single? Are you married? Do you have a girlfriend?" I politely shook my head 'no' per my usual routine. I discussed this phenomenon with Tiffany. I still felt ashamed and fearful of my admission while revealing myself to those around me. She told me, "You'll just know when you're ready one day, and then, that's it."

A week later, I woke up and began my morning routine. I filled a large bowl of cereal and made my way to my patio. The sun had just begun to rise above the horizon, and it welcomed in a beautiful spring morning in Colorado. I noticed an email from Tiffany. She sent me the song "Same Love" by Macklemore, a

Seattle based rapper. I opened it up, and played it on my cell phone. Macklemore proclaimed,

"It's human rights for everybody, there is no difference. Live on and be yourself...If you preach hate at the service those words aren't anointed. That holy water that you soak in has been poisoned. When everyone else is more comfortable remaining voiceless rather than fighting for humans that have had their rights stolen. No freedom till we're equal, damn right I support it."[12]

The song moved me. The lyrics inspired me. A straight male, mainstream artist in the rap industry nonetheless, boldly fought for gay people's rights. He didn't care what people thought of him or his image. He voiced his opinions and stood firmly behind them. The rap industry historically portrayed homophobia. Macklemore challenged that stance head-on.

I closed my eyes and reflected upon the song's lyrics. I became upset with myself. I questioned, "Just when is the right time, Adam? How can you be a 27 year old man, still meeting people in life with a screen over yourself and filter to them only what you want them to know?" I shoveled a few more spoonfuls of cereal into my mouth, and pressed repeat on the song. It finished. I looked up towards the sunrise. Everything seemed to make sense. I needed to overturn a decision that I repeatedly and habitually kept making in my life. I owed it to myself.

The day after I listened to the song, I sat in an office with my new boss Jennifer. "So, do you mind if I ask you something?" she said. "Are you married, dating, etc?"

I paused. With a slight hesitation I looked at her and said,

"You're from the east coast, right? Connecticut if I remember correctly?"

She nodded her head yes with a confused look upon her face.

"Ok, then you'll probably be ok with this. So I'm not... straight."

I left it at that. Her eyes slightly widened. Her hands came off the desk and she slapped them right back down. "Cool!" She proclaimed.

We both laughed and bonded over the moment. I shared the story of the song. It felt incredibly refreshing to share the real me with someone so soon after meeting them professionally. In that moment, I made the decision to start my new job with a blank slate and a self promise of honesty. We talked about my plan, and she pledged to stand behind me no matter what it took. In the coming weeks, my usual fear of the single/dating/girlfriend questions became replaced with excitement. I almost wished for people to ask me so that I could continue working upon my own self-worth and acceptance.

I decided to no longer wear a mask in the professional setting. The statements and answers to questions that once took hold of me like a prisoner now came out with feelings of liberation and joy. I forced myself to believe that I deserved to be where I was, regardless of my sexual orientation. The expression "I'm gay" slowly began to lose its power over me. The fear behind the statement's delivery incrementally faded away.

The Loss of a Friendship

While in college, my good friend Natalie became one of the first people to know that I was gay after Alex. Our friendship grew even closer because of it, and we shared some heartfelt conversations on the topic. She expressed her support for me, and told me just how much she loved me. She knew my deepest fears and many of my lifelong struggles firsthand, and helped me to get through some extremely difficult times.

Natalie originated from outside of the U.S., so her family rarely visited Siena College. My parents lovingly welcomed Natalie into our family as a home away from home. They referred to her as a daughter. They spoiled her with food and support, as they had done for years with many of my closest friends. When Natalie received a prestigious volleyball award, she elected my parents to receive the award with her on stage.

Something changed in Natalie after junior year. We discussed what happened with Kevin and I over the summer, and she seemed disconnected. She withheld her true opinions from me. I bluntly asked her what the issues were. She expressed uncertainty whether or not she could accept my 'lifestyle choices.' She claimed to not fully support them any longer. Natalie caught me completely off guard. Her words stung me hard.

"I'll stop 'choosing' to be gay, if you stop 'choosing' to be black," I said.

"It's not the same thing, Adam."

"It absolutely is," I said. "What have you ever done to determine your own skin color? And what have you ever done to determine your own sexuality? At what point in your life did you *choose* to be black, and at what point in your life did you *choose* to be straight? When did you consciously choose to be either one?"

We sat in silence. She stumbled through her eventual response. I interrupted her to pose a question.

"Marriage is extremely important to me, and one day I want to be married to a man that I love with all of my heart and want to spend the rest of my life with. With your religious beliefs aside, as one of my best friends, would you be in attendance at my wedding?"

She hesitated. Her hesitation alone killed me.

"Going to a gay wedding would symbolically mean that I support or approve of it. I don't know how that sits with me, or how it would be interpreted by my family."

My brain couldn't comprehend such a drastic switch in the opinions of a once best friend. We ended the conversation on that awkward note. During my senior year, we continued to hang out with our friends like normal. We found a way to reconcile, and found ways to still appreciate each other's friendship. However, I built up an imaginary wall when around her. I had slightly guarded and cautious conversations with her. I hated the feeling of a pretentious friendship. It lacked true authenticity, ease of interaction, and open and honest communication.

We revisited the conversation a few times before college ended. I struggled to remain entirely patient. Part of me couldn't help but to feel betrayed. One day, Natalie shared an "enlightening" video with me. The video showed "ex-gay" teenagers that were changed by prayer. It elaborated on how prayer groups and the Bible helped them change back to their 'natural form' to become heterosexuals. I watched confused, vulnerable, and brainwashed teenagers held down and forced to believe that they needed to change themselves. I felt extremely sad for those poor kids headed for a future filled with confusion, depression, and pain. I responded by sharing my side of the story, and my lifelong worth of painful and failed attempts to do so. I told her that it wasn't possible or healthy to do what she showed me. We arrived at a standstill. She saw the disagreement as a difference in opinion. I saw it as some of the most painful hurt that any friend had ever placed upon me.

After college, we slowly lost touch. Our online interactions and text message catch-ups were superficial at best. The more time I spent away from her, the more it bothered me how she left our friendship. As the days and years passed after school, I put less effort into maintaining whatever remained of our friendship.

One day, I randomly stumbled upon a post of hers online. She shared an article of a "Christian" man that claimed discrimination from gay business owners. He wanted the gay owners to make him products declaring that being gay is wrong and a sin. It quickly revealed itself as an extremely absurd and offensive article. It boasted claims that people from "the homosexual agenda" fought for, and used ridiculous statistics to try and drag gay people through the mud every which way it could. It cited how gay people died earlier in life, but not surprisingly, because of the amount of disease that "the gays" are susceptible to due to their extremely promiscuous lifestyles. The article even compared people fighting for gay marriage to ask why other people couldn't then fight for bestialities.

I couldn't continue on in my friendship with Natalie. My next steps weren't vindictive or out of spite. I removed her as a friend from Facebook. I sent her a lengthy message describing how it saddened me that she decided to share an article like that. I described how personally offensive it was to me. She knew that firsthand better than anyone. I thanked her for all of her years of friendship and let her know that I would forever cherish them, and love her as a person. I didn't have hatred for her, or an insurmountable obstacle that kept me from simply forgiving her. I just no longer had room for people like her in my life.

Meeting Logan

New Years 2014 rang in. Jake and I arrived at a standstill. I wasn't ready to take the next step forward with him. My head overtook my heart, and certain truths emerged from my once dormant subconscious. We were both so in love with the idea of being in love that we blindly overlooked some larger issues, such as our differences in personalities and hobbies. I struggled to believe that we genuinely enjoyed each other's constant company enough to have a chance at a healthy future. I stole time from not only my life, but worse yet from his.

I owed it to myself to listen to what my gut and heart told me. I owed just as much to him to be honest. I revisited many of my childhood and lifelong fears of never finding happiness for myself. The thoughts of breaking up with Jake tore my heart apart. His family still didn't acknowledge or support him. I pictured both of us single, and I couldn't fully fathom what life would be like for either of us. I cared for him deeply, but knew that I would only hurt him more if I continued to string him along.

Our apartment's lease had a few months left before expiring. I connected with a realtor in Denver and began to look at houses. Jake joined occasionally, but not always. One evening, I told Jake I needed to speak to him in the living room. I couldn't compose myself. While searching for the right words, I shook my head at my own ineptitude.

"I'm not sure I want to buy a house together," I said.

"I can tell," he said. "It's almost as if you wish I wasn't there even when I do join."

My emotional words started slurring together. After a few minutes of conversation I said, "I want to break up, Jake."

We locked eyes from across the room. Tears formed in his eyes and made their way down his face. We didn't speak for minutes as we both took in the weight of my statement.

"I know that we both love and care for each other deeply," I said. "I just don't think that we *like* each other enough to continue on as a couple."

"There's got to be a way we can reconcile the issue," he said. "We can start by going to the gym together, or do more trips on the weekends."

"It's not going to solve our personality conflicts. They haven't gone away since we've dated, and it's only become more evident once we've moved in together."

I stood behind my statements. Jake stared blankly at the floor. We conversed for more than an hour. I couldn't stop from crying. The thought of ripping away what we'd known so well for three years completely overwhelmed me. I began to hyperventilate and couldn't catch my breath. I walked to the bedroom. My bloodshot eyes blurred my vision and my lightheadedness skewed my balance. I sat down with my head between my knees. Jake soon followed.

"I can't keep talking," I said.

He handed me some Kleenex.

"Just focus upon your breathing," Jake said. "One slow breath at a time…"

We talked through the topic for a week. My emotions drained and my sleep became nonexistent. We attempted to heal each another and ourselves in the midst of our emotional train wreck. I sensed that Jake still held on to hope. I distanced myself physically and emotionally in order to detach. We agreed that when I landed a house in Denver, we would officially call it the end.

He searched for apartments. I signed a contract on a house and set a closing date. We arranged a moving company, and packed up our separate things. I pushed the last box into the moving van, and brushed off my hands. Jake stood at the apartment's door.

"So, can I give you a kiss or a hug?" he asked. "I don't know what to say."

"I think we say goodbye," I said.

I placed my water bottle down and wiped off the condensation from my palm. I held out my hand. He shook it.

"Goodbye, Jake."

"Goodbye, I guess."

I filled the rooms in my house with boxes and furniture. No matter how much stuff I jammed into each room, part of me still felt empty. My first home symbolized a new energy for me, but it scared me too. I was alone. I spoke to Tiffany and Nikki during my first week. They encouraged me to find myself again. I joined a gym down the street from my house. I put my feelers out for sports leagues and potential tournaments in Denver.

Almost two months passed by and I didn't have any luck. Gay Pride 2014 approached. The city of Denver prepared for a weekend-long celebration of gay rights commemorating social progress and change. I caught wind of a huge volleyball tournament on Saturday. I wanted to play badly, but had no direct "in" for a team or any friends that played. Chris, my best gay friend in Denver joked, "I don't know any 'sporty gays' Adam. Sorry!"

10:00pm approached on Friday night before the tournament. I put on jeans, a t-shirt, and laced up my sneakers to go out. "Ding!" my phone buzzed loudly with a text message. My coworker Elsa heard of a volleyball team at the tournament that needed a last-minute substitute. Elsa connected me with a girl named Sarah via text. Sarah explained what time the tournament was in the morning: 8:00am–5:00pm, arrive by 7:00am to set-up our area. Off came my shoes. I made a list of items for the following morning for food and drinks. I packed a cooler and lawn chairs in my Jeep.

I connected with Sarah and met the rest of our team. Our lawn chairs were situated next to a group of particularly good-looking guys. One guy really caught my eye. He had an amazing smile, a perfect body, and great athletic ability. I told my team that I would never have the opportunity to get to know someone like that, so I gave my secret crush a name, "Matty." We jokingly referred to him as that for the remainder of the day. Unfortunately, our paths never crossed, and I went home without having spoken to him.

On Sunday, I attended a party at the State Capitol. Multiple stages were set-up. The pounding music from concerts and celebrations filled the air. Out of the thousands in attendance packed in shoulder to shoulder, "Matty" appeared right near me. I took in a big gulp of my vodka soda, and a deep breath. I watched him interact with his friends for a few minutes, and slowly made my way towards him.

"Hey, didn't you play in the volleyball tournament yesterday?" I said.

"I did! Weren't you there as well?" he asked.

"I was," I said, surprised that he remembered me.

"My name is Logan, it's a pleasure to meet you."

"Likewise. My name is Adam."

Logan introduced me to his friends. The group politely welcomed me into their circle. We hoisted up our neon colored plastic cups with bendy straws and made a toast. Logan and I discussed sports. We talked about volleyball and tennis and perhaps getting together one day to play.

We kept in touch sporadically throughout the following couple of weeks. I learned that Logan was in the midst of ending a long term relationship. He didn't directly discuss it with me, but I empathized with him. I sensed his heartache of heading down the difficult path of breaking up with someone. We kept a slight distance with one another, to allow the space he needed. Logan's relationship ended. Feelings silently grew between us. We mutually agreed to not rush into anything and to take it slowly first as friends.

We went on a few nighttime ice cream runs, which felt like unofficial dates. Hailing from Longview, Texas, his southern manners never failed. He held every door open for me, as he did for others around us. When I attempted to pay, he placed my credit card behind his back, and provided his instead. His laughter and positivity shined through his genuinely kind personality. He seemed to always be smiling, and contagiously filled me with positive energy. We shared many of the same quotes from our favorite TV shows and movies that seemed to intersect as if we had grown up as longtime friends.

Logan worked as a personal trainer at a local gym. He got up at 4am to teach morning boot camp classes. He also attended nursing school full time. His previous experiences as a paramedic and a firefighter motivated him to continue in a career to help and care for others. He worked hard, studied hard, and never complained. His positivity drew me to him like a magnet. He made me laugh like a kid again. I innocently forgot the world's problems when we spent time together.

Later in the summer, I flew back home to New York for a week. Our nightly phone conversations began around ten minutes apiece. They quickly increased in time and surpassed an hour each evening. Logan coordinated to pick me up upon my return to Denver. He surprised me by waiting inside of the airport. He greeted me with a big hug, and grabbed my bags. On the way home he queued up my favorite song.

Inside the house, a giant poster board sat atop my kitchen counter. "Welcome home Adamazzzing!" It said. "I missed you!" A beautiful bouquet of yellow flowers stood next to the poster in a large vase. Thoughtful goodies and candy treats surrounded the flowers. I planted a big kiss square upon his lips. Goodbye single life, I thought to myself. Hook, line and sinker.

We officially began dating shortly thereafter. Our relationship felt natural to its core. We played sports together, hung out every night, and provided encouragement for each other's goals. We synergized effortlessly. For my 30th birthday the following spring, he took me down to Texas to meet his parents. Meeting my Texan boyfriend's parents intimidated me greatly. Logan held my hand on the plane and ensured me that they would love and accept me.

Upon arrival, his father Tommy shook my hand and told me how much he's heard about me. Jamie, Logan's mom, gave me a big hug and revealed her sweet Texan accent. They welcomed me into their home with open arms. The saying "everything is bigger in Texas" proved its truth after seeing their gorgeous home's ceiling height, cabinets in their kitchen, and furniture pieces around their home. They showed me around the town and treated us to dinner. I expressed my sincerest gratitude to them. Logan looked at me and said, "I told you that you'd have nothing to worry about!"

I felt like an outside observer to my own life. I couldn't help but to recall thoughts from childhood, convinced for years that I would forever be trapped inside of my secret misery. I never could have imagined the day of meeting my boyfriend's family as my genuine self. The progress fascinated me. Meeting Logan's parents unlocked a new aspect of happiness and acceptance in my life.

That next Christmas in Denver, Logan drove me to an unspecified location. My curiosity built with the passing of each mile. We arrived at a massive Christmas store. A 15-foot tall Santa stood on the roof welcoming us in. Ornaments hung upon every wall. Light strands illuminated fully decorated Christmas trees of all themes and sizes. Logan explained,

"I know how important your Dicken's Christmas Village is to you and your mom. You take such special time creating the beautiful scene. I thought that we could start a tradition of our own. I want to buy us our first house together, and then begin our very own collection."

I just about melted. My hands flew to my overjoyed face. At the back of the store, we assessed various pieces. One house in particular stood out to me.

"That one!" I proclaimed.

"Ok," he said. "That one it is!" An employee retrieved the piece for us from the back.

"Well, we can't just have a house without any people," he said.

We searched for the perfect people to compliment the house. We saw families holding presents, kids playing in the street, and various street vendors. Near the end of the case, we noticed a piece with two guys standing side by side. Their arms draped around each other's necks, and they held up pints of beer in a celebratory fashion. Logan and I chuckled. Our eyes slowly connected. We both proclaimed, "Gay!" and grabbed the piece, laughing our way through the store.

Logan placed the boxes in front of the cashier. He grabbed my hand. "Our first house," he said. He kissed my cheek. The cashier was looking. My lifelong reaction would have been to pull away. I never thought once to do so. The cashier scanned the house. Beep. She smiled, said the total, and Logan paid. "Here you are," she said, handing over the plastic bag. "Merry Christmas!"

Gay Marriage Legalized in Colorado and the Nation

On October 6th, 2014, images of rainbow flags filled the news headlines. Social Media outlets exploded. The Federal appeals court struck down bans against gay marriage in five states including Indiana, Oklahoma, Utah, Virginia and Wisconsin. Six other states (Colorado, Kansas, North Carolina, South Carolina, West Virginia and Wyoming) abided by the Court's ruling. With the Supreme Court's ruling, the U.S. finally pushed past 50% of its states legalizing marriage equality.

I wasn't awaiting such legislature to marry my significant other like many other couples in these states, yet the issue was extremely important to me. It represents one of the most important decisions anyone will ever make in their life. Extending the freedom to marry in these states meant that loving and committed couples could have access to the more than 1,100 federal benefits, rights, protections and responsibilities that marriage afforded a couple.

Prior to marriage equality, if one partner in an LGBT relationship got in an accident and was killed, their lifetime partner wouldn't have had any legal right to their benefits, their pensions, inherit assets or a shared home in absence of a will. They wouldn't have been considered next of kin for the purposes of hospital visitation and emergency medical decision-making. They wouldn't be able to cover their loved one or kids on their own health insurance plans. They would've been denied withdrawal rights and protective tax treatment given to spouses for retirement plans. They wouldn't even get bereavement time off from work if their partner died.[13]

A celebration took place upon the steps of the 10th Circuit Court of Appeals in Denver. I rushed home from work and biked downtown to witness a large gathering in front of the state court building. The building boasted massive white columns along the length of its front and had the year 1910 inscribed at its top. Rainbow flags, peace signs, and love equality messages filled the air. Spectators snapped pictures nonstop. Colorado Governor John Hickenlooper attended. Perched on top of the building's impressive staircase with a microphone in hand, Governor Hickenlooper shared, "Today marks a historic day on the march toward marital equality. While there are a few more steps in the process, we are that much closer to declaring marriage equality for all Coloradans."[14]

I listened to heartfelt stories of long-time and loving couples that anxiously awaited to see this day in their lifetimes. Representatives from the NAACP and leaders of the Latino community voiced their approval, reflecting upon the importance to overcome all discrimination. A Reverend Dr. sported a multi-colored stole around her neck. She voiced her unending support of marriage equality and of love. She disapproved and disbelieved the many churches and religious leaders who spent their efforts fighting against gay people. She declared that God is love and love is God, and those that preach differently are merely fighting for their own agendas. Her words struck me with vigor. I dreamed of getting married as a kid. I never thought it would be possible in my lifetime to actually do so.

A woman approached the stand. Her voice slightly quivered as she fought back tears. She declared, "The fight is not over." In her home state of Ohio, she spoke about her friend Shannon who came out at work, and got fired from her job. She shared another story of when her friends, a gay couple of 10 years, were unjustly fired from their jobs after adopting a child. She spoke about the legal discrimination that still happened every single day around the U.S. She spoke about a Dr. that recently refused to treat a baby of a gay couple after "praying over the issue." Information packets were distributed encouraging the continued push for LGBT advocacy and equality.

Nine short months later on June 26th, 2015, the Supreme Court ruled in favor of same sex marriage nationwide. The United States became the 21st country in the world to do so. Justice Anthony Kennedy wrote for the majority of the Supreme Court and stated, "No union is more profound than marriage, for it embodies the highest ideals of love, fidelity, devotion, sacrifice and family…in forming a marital union, two people become something greater than they once were."[15] I became engrossed in social media outlets and the news reports.

Timelines illustrated gay rights history in America. The visible progression humbled me. President Hoover and the FBI used to keep lists of homosexuals on file to ensure that gay people couldn't teach or serve in the government. Gay people were expelled from universities, publicly harassed and beaten, imprisoned, and thrown into mental hospitals. In the 1960's, the government shut down gay businesses, exposing their clientele in local newspapers. LGBT activists couldn't take it anymore. The Stone Wall Riots in New York City ignited the fire for LGBT rights across America in 1969. For decades, brave men and women stood up and fought for equality. America's opinion on gay rights slowly transformed. Marriage equality represented the biggest shift in American history during my lifetime regarding LGBT rights.

Certain friends and family members rejoiced with me. Other's opposed the ruling with outrage. My cousin Gina texted me, "I'm so happy for equality at last!" One of my Aunts posted on Facebook in opposition. She claimed that businesses should have the right to deny gay weddings. The division spread nationwide. Some businesses opened their doors with messages of love and equality while others refused to do so. A county clerk in Kentucky refused marriage licenses, claiming it was against her religious beliefs. Her social and political followers expressed the urgency to keep marriage "traditional" in the United States, and to continue suppressing LGBT rights.

In the repeating pattern of our nation and world's past, personal discriminations were once again verified by exploiting the Bible. Those fighting against the law of marriage equality used the scapegoat term of 'traditional marriage' to hide behind. However, traditional marriage in the Bible occurred when families allied to benefit land, money, and power. Traditional marriage in the Bible describes pre-arranged marriages, sometimes involving incest. Famous Biblical characters lived out lives of polygamy, some with hundreds of wives. Woman's roles are distinctly drawn out and include submission to husbands, bans for any leadership or power at home or within society, and strict rules to stay at home and to stay quiet. People hypocritically chose which Bible verses, and even which societal laws, to abide by. They utilized religion as a mechanism for their ongoing excuses to discriminate.

My disappointment and frustrations grew with those who continued working to oppress my rights. Their words echoed loudly in my mind. I rehearsed statements to make and messages to share online. However, I silenced my desires to respond. I refused to engage with people spreading messages of hate. I didn't reply to my family or friend's posts online that refuted marriage equality. I focused upon the positives, and upon justice and equality. I became overwhelmed with thankfulness towards those who passionately advocated for my very rights even before my birth. I researched and joined additional statewide and nationwide organizations online to continue the fight for LGBT equality.

Marriage as we know it today isn't about land, property, wealth, or guaranteeing family prominence or future relationships as it once was. Marriage has transcended into a true societal privilege. It encompasses mutual love, respect, attraction, and mutual division of labor and responsibility for the relationship. Marriage equality doesn't affect anyone's religious beliefs or personal opinions, nor their church's beliefs, regulations, or requirements to perform weddings or approve of them. Everyone deserves the equal right to commit and dedicate himself or herself to someone whom they love in this lifetime.

The Adventure Of A Lifetime

Logan took me out to a nice Italian dinner for my 31st birthday in Denver. He knew my comfort food. Italian artwork hung on Florentine-themed brick and stucco walls. Beautiful stone columns formed arches around its doorways. The entire wait staff smiled as they served us. Rustic bread, hearty entrees, and glasses of Italian wine filled our table. We excitedly talked about our spring plans and upcoming summer together. We spoke about our families, a subject dear to both of our hearts. The delicious food filled us to the brim. We resisted the urges for dessert, until the temptation of pistachio gelato set in. Our friendly waiter presented us a bowl of the delectable treat, complete with a birthday candle in its center.

"You've got to make a wish!" Logan said.

I closed my eyes and blew out the candle. I smiled and couldn't stop staring across the table at Logan. We combated our spoons in the gelato, and Logan relinquished the last few bites. I turned the bowl on its side and scooped out every last ounce. We had plans with our friend Sarah, and made our way to meet her out for a celebratory birthday drink. On the way past our house, Logan stopped.

"I have one more birthday present for you," he said.

Inside, Logan instructed me to stand in the living room with my eyes closed. He went to retrieve a gift from the basement. My curiosity built. He said, "I'm coming up, don't turn around yet!"

I heard large wheels coming towards me on the hardwood floor. "Luggage?" I asked.

"Ok. Turn around," he said.

A large black luggage had two bows on top of it, and a letter neatly folded within its handle. We hugged. I thanked him for the beautiful luggage. I needed a new suitcase badly. I opened the letter. Hand written, it filled an entire page. It depicted our relationship for the past year and a half full of love, growth, and friendship. It hinted at the luggage being symbolic for our many adventures. Logan appeared a little nervous. I thought nothing of it. Reading aloud, I finished the last few sentences, "I have planned yet another adventure for us, if you are willing to take it with me. It will be hard at times, but also the most amazing love filled adventure that we have total control of. Walking or running, but always hand in hand, side by side, Adam James Mastroianni…"

Logan reached into his back pocket. Tears formed in his eyes and his face turned slightly red. He dropped down to one knee, and held up a beautiful gold wedding band.

"Will you marry me?" he asked.

My hands covered my face in surprise.

"Yes!" I proclaimed. "Yessss!"

He got up off of his knee and slid the ring onto my ring finger. It fit perfectly. I dreamed of the exact ring. We embraced one another and buried our tears of joy into each other's shoulder. I blinked hard a few times and let out a scream of joy. The ring shined bright. Logan shined brighter. I knew that there was nobody else in the entire world that I would rather spend my life with.

"Are you serious?!" I asked him repeatedly.

He nodded his head yes while gently wiping away a tear. The ever-planner and manager that I am, I had planned to propose to him in the summer or fall. He snuck right up on me and caught me with a complete and joyous surprise. We hugged our loving dog Shadow who approached us with kisses and her wagging tail. I thought of my family. I called home, and they put me on speakerphone.

"We all knew," they said. "Logan called last week to ask for our blessing. We have been anxiously awaiting to hear from you tonight!"

I laughed and then silently cried. They expressed their deepest love and support. I thanked God for giving me life's best blessing through Logan, true and unconditional love. I thanked Logan for making me feel like the most loved, appreciated, and special guy in the entire world. I wanted to text and call my best friends immediately. Logan encouraged us to get going, as to not let Sarah wait too long for us at the bar.

"She'll be just fine!" I said. "We just got engaged! She can wait a couple more minutes while I take a few pictures and make some calls."

Logan waited patiently. He accepted my numerous hugs every time my eyes glanced past my left ring finger and I let out a shriek of excitement. He shut the kitchen lights.

"Come on, love. We told her 8pm and it's already 8:30. Let's make our way there."

Upon arrival, he held the door open for me. My eyes glanced around the bar, but I couldn't find Sarah. In the back of the bar in a separate room, I saw my friend Josh.

"Logan, Josh is here! What are the chances? Let's go and say hi."

The rest of the room and a large table came into view. Ten of my closest friends in Denver sat around the table and welcomed us in. I planted a big kiss upon Logan's cheek.

"You little stinker!" I proclaimed.

I introduced my new ring and my new fiancé to everyone, including our waiter. We uncorked champagne bottles. Our friends filled us with loving words, and plenty of laughter. I couldn't wait to tell the rest of the world. When Liz lifted her camera for pictures, I placed the ring front and center in every one of them. Time stopped each time reality set in. We texted and called our best friends and family members. Loving words filled the night's air from friends and family both near and far.

Logan gently held my hand under the table. It felt like home. The man of my dreams sat next to me smiling. Logan's eyes smiled the most genuine smile I'd ever seen. Our friends treated us the entire night. After champagne and wine toasts at another bar, we grabbed one final drink. Our good friends Sarah and Heather rang in the final toasts of the evening. The most special and memorable night of my life soon came to a close. The best chapter of my life, however, had only just begun.

A Call For Action

The 2014 winter Olympics in Russia brought worldwide attention to LGBT rights. Harsh anti-gay laws preceded the Games' excitement. Russia introduced banning "homosexual propaganda" nationwide. The law passed, along with a law that banned "propaganda of nontraditional sexual relations," imposing hefty fines for providing information about the LGBT community to minors, in addition to holding any gay pride rallies or demonstrations.

Lawmakers in Russia accused LGBT people of decreasing Russia's already low birth rates. They barred LGBT citizens from government jobs, forced them to undergo medical treatment, and attempted to exile them. An executive on a government run television network said on a nationally televised talk show that gays should be prohibited from "donating blood, sperm, and organs for transplants, while after their death their hearts should be burned or buried."[16] Violent anti-LGBT hate crimes and murders went unpunished or received minimal sentencing.

Unfortunately, the laws in Russia are not that uncommon throughout the world. Nations in the Americas, Oceania, Africa, Asia and the Middle East maintain anti-gay laws that result in various punishments from fines to short- and life-long prison sentences, hard labor, forced psychiatric treatment, banishment, whippings, and even death.[17] As of 2015, same-sex sexual acts between consenting adults is still criminalized in 75 countries around the world. Eight nations still officially sentence homosexuality with the death penalty.

More equality does not come with relinquishing the fight for equality. Currently, marriage equality exists in only 9% of United Nations member states.[18] It is still legal to discriminate against LGBT people in the workplace in two-thirds of the world. I have friends that are still completely closeted due to their overwhelming fears of their family and society.

Year after year, representative to the proportion of various minority groups, data shows that LGBT minorities are far more likely than any other group to be victims of violent hate crimes.[19] In American schools, 9 out of 10 LGBT youth report being bullied because of their sexual orientation, and 25% of these students report being physically assaulted. Sixty-four percent of LGBT students said that homophobic remarks like "dyke" and "faggot" are heard frequently or often, with 51% stating that their teachers or staff use homophobic remarks as well.[20]

With new legislation and rights being passed, and as gay rights issues continue to be brought forth in headlines and discussed publicly, the coming out age has dropped from post-college age in the 1990s to around 16 years old in 2015.[21] Kids are still fully reliant economically on their parents at this age. Parents are commonly kicking kids out of their homes for being gay. Although those who identify as LGBT make up roughly 4-5% of the youth population, they make up a staggering 40% of the homeless youth population.

The Center for American Progress reports that there are currently between 320,000 to 400,000 homeless LGBT youths in the United States. Every four hours an LGBT homeless youth dies in the streets from freezing to death, a drug overdose, or a deadly assault.[22] Most tragically, conservative estimates show that 1,500 gay and lesbian youth take their own lives each year.

As an adolescent, I too questioned if I deserved the same rights as those around me. No matter the classifications, each person matters, and each person deserves an equal shot at finding their own happiness in life both personally and professionally. We must bestow upon each child an equal chance at success, free from intolerance and prejudice. Gay rights shouldn't be gay rights – they are simply human rights. We must continue the surge for progress.

It took Ellen DeGeneres three years to find a job after coming out publicly. Years later, Forbes named Ellen as the 10th most powerful woman in the world. She has become one of the driving forces behind the growing acceptance of the LGBT community in America. Ellen stands for treating others the way you wish to be treated, and is the epitome of the statement "Promote what you love instead of bashing what you hate" (*author unknown*). She has used her fame and her incredible humanitarian efforts to relentlessly bring forth positivity to the world. Ellen helped pave the way for me and for so many others, by inspiring people worldwide to reach for their dreams by being honest and true to themselves.

Judy and Dennis Shepard fought for eleven long years to get sexual orientation added into the nation's vitally important hate-crime laws. In 2009, the Shepards and Congress passed the Matthew Shepard & James Byrd Jr. Hate Crimes Prevention Act. The Shepard's foundation, the Matthew Shepard Foundation, empowers individuals to embrace human dignity and diversity. They strive to replace hate with understanding, compassion and acceptance, and have spoken at countless schools, organizations, and communities all across the nation.

We must start by challenging our own or other's stereotypes, and by opening up our minds to allow for acceptance of diversity. We must start by telling one person that the word "gay" should not be used with negative implications. We must educate our kids on differences in people within society before they are subjected to peer pressures in school, which can result in bullying and intolerance. We don't have to fully agree with or understand everyone around us, but we must look to eliminate deeply instilled prejudices and miseducations towards an entire group of people.

Change in people's perceptions, attitudes, beliefs, and actions is possible. People's lives so desperately depend upon it. If you're struggling to find meaning and understanding in life, find the strength to hold on. It will get better. If you are in need of help, would like to learn how to take a stand against hate, or to find out how you too can join the fight for human equality, please see the list of resources immediately following the Conclusion in **Appendix A**.

Conclusion

LGBT people have had and continue to have an incredible amount of influence and inspiration to the products, possessions, entertainment, inventions, and scientific and medical discoveries that all of us use and depend upon each and every day. To scratch the surface: Alan Turing was gay, the man that British Prime Minister Winston Churchill acclaimed as ending WWII. Tim Cook is gay, the CEO of the world's largest and most valuable company, Apple. My good friend Chris is gay, the Chief Medical Officer of the nation's largest network of healthcare clinics. Our work is for our entire country's benefit. It is not partitioned by class or applicable to an "elite" race or "preferred" sexuality. We inarguably deserve to have the same societal rights, privileges, and protections, as does every American.

It is both hurtful and unfounded to believe homosexuality is a choice. Gay people never chose to face discrimination, harassment, hatred, and even hate crimes and murder. My genetic makeup and who I am uniquely belongs to me as much as my fingerprints do. An LGBT person may not be "normal" to someone that is straight, because it's different. It's different like a woman is from a man, or a black person is from a white person, or a tall person is from a small person. But being different doesn't need to mean that it's wrong. It just means that it's different.

Religiously, thousands of belief systems exist in the world. No single person has the one true answer. Christians follow the teachings of Jesus. He preached unconditional love above all else, and commanded that we treat each and every person equally and not to judge one another. These teachings are paramount to Christianity, yet many Christians commonly overlook them. Throughout history and still in present day, Christians destroy Christianity by placing undue judgment upon others. False Christians have discriminated against countless people and entire groups both religiously and secularly. We must put an end to this unjust pattern in our culture.

In my 31 years on this planet, I have learned quite a few things in regards to the meaning and purpose of life. I've learned that sometimes the greatest moments of building character and strength come from the hardest failures or setbacks in life. I've learned that attitude is a vital decision that we can choose to make each and every day. People will not remember all of the things that you said or did in life, but they will always remember how you made them feel. Maintain a focus upon giving back to others, and in doing so realize the deep satisfaction that it brings. And I've learned the most important characteristic in life that we have as a people is both intangible and internal. It's the love, the meaning, and the intentions that reside from within our hearts.

I don't know why I was born gay. Perhaps it was so that one day I could adopt children that otherwise may have spent their lives in foster homes and to provide them with a better future. Perhaps it was to hopefully help even just one person that was born in the same boat while here on this earth and felt hopeless for their future. All I know is that just like everyone else, God has given me a unique toolkit and I am trying to do the best I can with it. No matter what circumstances surround us in life amidst tragedy and triumph, pain and pleasure, chaos and calm, and disappointment and accomplishment, we must nurture ourselves and our lives and consciously work to enrich those lives around us.

Words cannot express my thankfulness to my family and friends who have helped me through both my darkest and brightest days. God has truly blessed me by placing all of your incredible love and support in my life. I am deeply appreciative and full of gratitude for the readers of this book, for taking the time to read my story. I am even more so thankful for your purchase as it solidifies a free copy to be donated to a high school, church, homeless shelter, or organization around the United States. Your support and belief in equality and fairness can and will bring about a better future for us all, even if it starts with reaching just one person.

Each day we are given unique opportunities to have an immediate impact upon those around us. We must challenge ourselves to live our lives free from hypocrisy and exclusion, and full of love and inclusion. Whether we start by helping one person in need, challenge one long standing perception or prejudice, or have one ambitious goal to bring about equality and change, we can all move forward towards creating a better society and world together. We must start somewhere. We just need to Start With One.

Appendix A:

Are you in need of help? Do you want to learn how to provide resources, education, or join a cause or donate to one? Start here.

NEED HELP?

The Trevor Project: www.thetrevorproject.org - the leading national organization providing crisis intervention and suicide prevention service to LGBTQ youth. Confidential help is available 24/7. Dial: 1-866-488-7386.

GALIP Foundation (God's Agape Love (put) Into Practice): www.gaychurch.org - the world's largest, most comprehensive LGBT Christian Affirming Church Directory available in the world.

National Coalition For The Homeless: www.nationalhomeless.org - homeless persons or soon to be homeless people, contact the National Switchboard. For help, dial 1-800-621-4000, or email info@nationalhomeless.org with the name of your city and state.

GLBT National Help Center: www.glbthotline.org - organization providing a safe environment on the phone or internet for people of all ages for peer-support, helping youth and adults with coming-out issues, family concerns, and much more. GLBT National Hotline: (toll-free & confidential): 1-888-843-4564, email: help@GLBThotline.org

GLBT National Resource Database: www.GLBTnearme.org - The largest collection of GLBT resources on the web of more than 15,000 resources. Search by zip code, and sort by 26 categories including social and support resources, community centers, youth groups, and much more.

National Suicide Prevention Lifeline:
www.suicidepreventionlifeline.org - providing free and confidential
emotional support to people in suicidal crisis or emotional distress
24 hours a day, 7 days a week. Call: 1-800-273-8255.

It Gets Better Project: www.itgetsbetter.org - communicating to
LGBT youth around the world that it gets better, and to create and
inspire the changes needed to make it better for them.

WANT TO GET INVOLVED?

Matthew Shepard Foundation: www.matthewshepard.org - empowering individuals to embrace human dignity and diversity through outreach, advocacy and resource programs. Focuses to replace hate with understanding, compassion and acceptance.

Human Rights Campaign: www.hrc.org - the largest civil rights organization working to achieve equality for LGBT Americans, envisioning a world where LGBT people are embraced as full members of society at home, at work, and in every community.

The National LGBTQ Task Force: www.thetaskforce.org - the country's oldest national LGBTQ advocacy group, working to advance full freedom, justice, and equality for LGBTQ people.

Parents, Families, Friends, and Allies United with LGBTQ People (PFLAG): community.pflag.org - the nation's largest family and ally organization committed to advancing equality and full societal affirmation of LGBTQ people through support, education, and advocacy.

Stop Bullying: www.stopbullying.gov - provides information for parents, educators, community, teens, and kids on what bullying is, what cyber bullying is, who is at risk, and how you can prevent and respond to bullying.

International Lesbian, Gay, Bisexual, Trans and Intersex Association (ILGA): www.ilga.org - a worldwide federation dedicated to achieving equal rights for LGBTI people, and liberating LGBTI people from all forms of discrimination.

Point Foundation, The National LGBTQ Scholarship Fund: www.pointfoundation.org - the nation's largest scholarship-granting organization for LGBTQ students, empowering LGBTQ students to achieve their full academic and leadership potential. Toll-free: 1-866-397-6468.

If you have purchased this book online, please be sure to share your feedback by leaving a review! I would love to hear what you thought about the work.

References

[1] Chen, J. (2015, October 23). Ellen DeGeneres on Coming Out as Gay: "I Didn't Think I Was Going to Come Out, Period" US Weekly.

[2] Most Common Same-sex Confusion in the Bible. (2016). Retrieved January, 2016, from www.ourspiritnow.org

[3] White, M., Rev. Dr. (1998, January 1). What the Bible Says - And Doesn't Say - About Homosexuality. 17-18.

[4] Stocker, A. (2013, August 19). The Craziest Statistic You'll Read About North American Missions.

[5] Griffith, W. (2009, July 24). Know Your Bible? Many Christians Don't. Retrieved October, 2015, from www.cbn.com

[6] Most American Christians Do Not Believe that Satan or the Holy Spirit Exist. (2009, April 13). Retrieved October, 2015, from www.barna.org

[7] White, M., Rev. Dr. (1998, January 1). What the Bible Says - And Doesn't Say - About Homosexuality.

[8] Fantoli, A. (2005). The Disputed Injunction and its Role in Galileo's Trial. In McMullin (2005, pp. 117–149).

[9] Augustine of Hippo (408). De Genesi ad literam 1:19–20, Chapt. 19.

[10] American Psychological Association. (2008). Answers to your questions: For a better understanding of sexual orientation and homosexuality. Washington, DC. Retrieved April, 2014, from www.apa.org/topics/sorientation.pdf

[11] Goebbels, J. (2015). Joseph Goebbels Quotes. Retrieved February 16, 2016, from en.thinkexist.com

[12] Macklemore & Lewis, R. (2016). Macklemore Lyrics. Retrieved November 18, 2014, from www.azlyrics.com

[13] Wolfson, E. Why Marriage Matters, Appendix B. Retrieved October, 2015, from www.freedomtomarry.org

[14] Gov. Hickenlooper's Statement on U.S. Supreme Court Decision to Deny Ruling On Same-Sex Marriage. (2014, October 6). Retrieved April 5, 2016, from www.colorado.gov

[15] Vogue, A. D., & Diamond, J. (2015, June 27). Supreme Court rules in favor of same-sex marriage nationwide. Retrieved November, 2015, from www.cnn.com

[16] The Associated Press. (2013, January 21). Russia pushes ban on 'homosexual propaganda,' including public kissing by same-sex couples. Retrieved February, 2014, from www.nydailynews.com

[17] Jones, S. (2013, August 9). 76 Countries Where Anti-Gay Laws Are As Bad As Or Worse Than Russia's. Retrieved February, 2015, from www.buzzfeed.com

[18] International Lesbian, Gay, Bisexual, Trans and Intersex Association (May 2015) Carroll, A. & Itaborahy, L.P. State Sponsored Homophobia 2015: A world survey of laws: criminalization, protection and recognition of same-sex love.

[19] Potok, M. (2011, February 27). Comparing the rate of victimization for gays and lesbians to that of other groups. Retrieved December, 2014, from www.splcenter.org

[20] Gay Bullying Statistics. (2015, August). Retrieved September, 2015, from www.bullyingstatistics.org

[21] Morries, A. (2014, September 3). The Forsaken: A Rising Number of Homeless Gay Teens Are Being Cast Out by Religious Families. RollingStone.

[22] Ibid.

Made in the USA
Columbia, SC
28 May 2018